ENGLISH LANGUAG

A Blueprint fo
Key Stage 3

David and Helen Orme

Stanley Thornes (Publishers) Ltd

First published in 1995 by:
Stanley Thornes (Publishers) Ltd
Ellenborough House
Wellington Street
CHELTENHAM GL50 1YW
England

96 97 98 99 00 / 10 9 8 7 6 5 4 3

A catalogue record for this book is available from the British Library.

ISBN 0–7487–1930–X

Design and Layout by D&J Hunter (Beckenham)
Printed and bound in Great Britain at Ashford Colour Press, Gosport

CONTENTS

ACKNOWLEDGEMENTS

The authors and publishers are grateful to the following for permission to reproduce poems, letters and extracts: Moira Andrew, 'Night Monster', pp.23 and 29; Stan Barstow, 'Joby', extract reproduced on p.89 by permission of Michael Joseph Ltd; John Kirkbride, 'In Reply to Your Advertisement', Scholastic Publications Ltd 1989 – reproduced on p.62; Sue Limb, 'Me Jane', Orchard Books, extract reproduced on p.88; Judith Nicolls, 'First Day at School' pp.22 and 28.

Every effort has been made to contact copyright holders and we apologise if any have been overlooked.

INTRODUCTION

These photocopiable materials are designed for students at Key Stage 3. Although many of the worksheets have an application right across the ability range, the focus is on students working at levels 3 to 6. Much of the material has been designed particularly for withdrawal groups, and individuals and groups working in a mainstream class with a support teacher.

STRUCTURE OF THE MATERIALS

The photocopiable format allows this material to be used very flexibly and it is not envisaged that students will work through it from cover to cover. The book is organised according to the writing process itself:

- Starters
- Drafting
- Writing forms
- Writing styles
- Language patterns
- Proof reading
- Word processing
- Assessment.

The writing process itself is flexible, and will be structured according to the imperatives of the particular piece of writing. Very often the determination of form (short story, for example) will come first. All the worksheets can be used on a stand alone basis, or can be linked together to provide a structured and progressive series of tasks. A route for short story writing, for example, might be **Story types** (looking at genre) **Story plots** and/or **Story-boards**, **Story 1 and 2**, **Interesting characters**, and **Redrafting 1 – Stories**. If required, an extra loop could be inserted to look at **"and"**, **Direct speech** and **First person – Using 'I'** (work on first person writing). Proof reading and spelling suggestions might complete the task. Probably the teacher will not want to use all of these, but will make a selection based on the specific task, and the needs of the students. If the task is more concerned with the form for direct speech, **Punctuation 4 – "and"** might be the first worksheet, followed by **Direct-speech**. Clear links between the sheets are shown in the teacher's notes.

WORKING WITH THE SHEETS

The teacher's notes suggest appropriate ways for students to tackle the sheets, and how the task may be differentiated for students of differing abilities. An important principle is that differentiation is not just about different worksheets. Some students may have no problem with taking a copy of a page home and completing it for a homework assignment. Others may need to work through it with a support teacher acting as a scribe. All the sheets require some preparation, often in the form of a preliminary discussion with the class or group. Students should not be expected to tackle the pages 'cold'. Some pages can work well as a pair or group task – others specifically require this approach.

Most sheets are for writing on, but not all take the same approach. Some have exercises, some 'tick boxes', some are for notes and drafts, some for more finished pieces of work. In some cases, work needs to be continued over the sheet or on a further sheet of paper. In many cases the teacher may prefer all the written work to be done on separate sheets of paper, so that the photocopy sheets can be filed and reused. It is worth contemplating, however, whether the financial saving is worth the extra administration involved in filing large numbers of pieces of paper.

Word processing

Three pages are devoted to word processing and desk top publishing, appropriate for any system in use in school. An attractive final presentation is a real confidence booster to less able students, and the word processor can bring a professional appearance to their work. In addition, the wide range of software now available can broaden the scope of many of the tasks here. It is a simple task to improvise, draft, redraft and print out a short playscript, for example. Other software provides templates to produce newspapers or posters. Improved print hardware such as colour, bubblejet and laser printers can give superb results for a special piece of work.

Assessment

A series of assessment pages are included at the end. Their position here does not imply that assessment is always the final part of the writing process, or that a written value judgement is the only way that writing can be assessed. The pages allow students, however, to reflect on the work they have done, and on the process by which the work came about.

The pages can be used in two other ways:

1 For students, individually or collaboratively, to write about other material, either from printed sources or produced by a writing partner

2 For the teacher to use to give guidance to students about a particular piece of written work.

David and Helen Orme

Section 1 Section

Starters

These pages provide help with the difficult business of getting started, providing structures for the initial stages of planning a piece of writing. For the most able children these processes may well come naturally, but average and below average achievers often lack the confidence to think a piece of work through before embarking on it.

Using the worksheets

Brainstorming 1 and 2

Objective: Gathering material for writing.
Students: If students are unfamiliar with the idea of brainstorming it is recommended that the process should be worked through first as a group activity, with the teacher acting as a scribe, perhaps using the chalkboard.
Notes: Most youngsters, if left to their own devices, will launch into a piece of writing without the least idea of where it is going. These brainstorm pages show one, fairly formalised, way of gathering observations and experiences. The section on word pictures will require particular attention, and further work may need to be done on simile and metaphor, without necessarily using these words.
Follow up: The brainstorm material produced can be worked up into poems or pieces of descriptive prose. Stress that the students need to select from the material available, and should not attempt to use it all.
Linked pages: Word pictures p.6, Describing places 1 and 2 p.67 and 68. Brainstorming 2 p.5 can be used to start off many of the writing tasks in these materials.

Word pictures

Objective: To take the process of observation one stage further, using simile and metaphor.
Students: Group discussion followed by individual writing.
Notes: This sheet encourages students to look at the world in their own unique way. Look for other simple examples of metaphor and simile in poems and descriptive writing. Riddle writing is a useful and entertaining exercise in which the reader has to guess what is being described.
Follow up: Further 'word picture' poems, to be extended and drafted.
Linked pages: Word choice 2 p.29, More word pictures p.33, Poetry 1, 2, 4, pp.52-3, 55.

Facts and opinions

Objective: To extract information from a passage and reproduce it in note form; to identify different qualities of information, i.e. fact and supposition.
Students: Individual, pair or group work.
Notes: The initial stage of highlighting or underlining is a valuable skill which makes note writing much easier. The page provides a model for teachers to make up their own materials by blanking out the text and replacing it with a new passage.
Differentiation: The sheet can be worked on a question and answer basis with a support teacher highlighting and scribing.
Linked pages: Working on notes p.8, Redrafting 2 – Prose p.35, Describing places 1 – Planning it out p.67.

Working on notes

Objectives: To sort out and rationalise information, cutting out irrelevancies; to produce a paragraph of connected writing, appropriately sequenced.
Students: Individual writing following a group discussion.
Notes: Ensure that students are aware of the subject of the sheet – penguins. (For a more testing exercise, you could mask out the illustration of the penguin before photocopying the worksheet.) Encourage them to mark up the notes by crossing out irrelevancies, drawing lines to link material and adding numbers to show an order for the paragraph.
Differentiation: This page can be used for a class/group exercise led by a teacher/support teacher.
Linked pages: Facts and opinions p.7, Listening and note making 1 and 2 pp.9 and 10, Redrafting 2 – Prose p.35.

Listening and note making 1 and 2

Objective: To develop the following skills: silent reading and reading aloud; careful listening; retaining and recalling information; ordering information.
Students: Pair work.
Notes: The reader will need to work on a different task once he or she has read out the passage. The writer cannot be expected to read and prepare a piece on a different subject before attempting to recall the information he or she has heard.
Differentiation: Other approaches are possible such as student/support teacher, teacher/group.
Linked pages: Facts and opinions p.7, Working on notes p.8, Redrafting 2 – Prose p.35.

Story types

Objective: To introduce a range of fictional genres and look at their contents.
Students: Class group discussion followed by individual work.
Notes: The pictures on the sheet illustrate the general theme of the genre rather than the specific incident in the text. This sheet requires far more class/individual discussion than the others in this section. Talk about reading preferences, particular favourite books.
Follow up: Book reviews, reports, blurbs, jackets.
Linked pages: Story-boards 1 and 2 pp.18 and 19, Story plots 1 – Climaxes p.16, Redrafting 1 – Stories p.34, Story 1 and 2 pp.50 and 51.

Story telling true stories

Objective: To develop personal narratives using a story-telling approach.
Students: Pair work.
Notes: Introduce the topic by talking about the sorts of incidents mentioned in the first paragraph, perhaps with an anecdote of your own. When the students have told each other their stories, ask them to choose one and complete the story report. Encourage the use of direct speech.
Differentiation: This sheet can work well on a one to one basis with a support teacher.
Follow up: The story can be worked up into a a few paragraphs of paired writing.
Linked pages: Direct speech p.48, Story-boards pp.18, Redrafting 1 – Stories p.34, Autobiography 2 p.81, Personal writing p.88.

Interesting characters 1, 2 and 3

Objective: To provide a format for developing writing about people, real or imaginary.
Students: Individual writing.
Notes: Encourage students to see that a description is far more than simply what a character looks like, and that special characteristics and personal anecdotes tell an enormous amount about a person. This exercise can easily turn into an attack on people and the teacher may like to stipulate that true characters must be ones that the student likes! Characters 3 offers more characters for the character file.
Follow up: The character descriptions can be used with the story-board and plot planning sheets to develop story writing.
Linked pages: Interesting characters 3 p.15, Biography 1 and 2 pp.82 and 83.

Story plots 1 and 2

Objective: To demonstrate two strategies for narrative structure, one for an adventure-type story which builds up to a climax or resolution and another which involves conflict.
Students: Individual work, perhaps following a group planning session.
Notes: Encourage students to think about first and third person writing as possibilities. The conflict sheet will require attention to writing in direct speech.
Follow up: Writing the actual stories, or using the material from the story-board activity for scripting or for improvised drama.
Linked pages: First person – Using 'I' p.108, Direct speech p.48, Story-boards 1 and 2 pp.18

and 19, Redrafting 1 – Stories p.34, Punctuation 4 – "and" p.122, Playscript 1 p.56.

STORY-BOARDS 1 AND 2

Objective: To introduce a different approach to building narratives.
Students: Pair work.
Notes: The first sheet has an 'alternative ending' option for discussion. Story-boards using pictures can be an introduction to comic book writing. The story outline produced on Sheet 2 can be worked up into paired or individual writing, or used for scripting.
Differentiation: Work on a group story with the teacher/support teacher acting as scribe.
Linked pages: Story plots 1 and 2 pp.16 and 17, Redrafting 1 – Stories p.34, Playscript 1 p.56.

IN MY OPINION 1 AND 2

Objective: To offer a strategy for setting out beliefs or opinions and countering opposing arguments.
Students: Class discussion (Sheet 1); individual work (Sheet 2).
Differentiation: The pages can be simplified by asking for just two reasons, cutting the opposing arguments, or by filling it in with a teacher/support teacher scribing and asking questions.
Linked pages: Persuasion 2 – Junk food p.75.

Brainstorming 1

When you brainstorm, you gather up as many words and ideas as you can for your piece of writing. You don't have to use all of your ideas. Save up the ones you are not using for another time.

A writer made this brainstorm after a walk in the park. Use the words and ideas in a piece of writing of your own. Add your own ideas - use your imagination!

IN THE PARK

Seeing, colour

trees, grass, many shades of green

bright clothes, flower beds

tall buildings around the park

grey, red brick

Touching, feeling

sun and wind on my face

put my hand in pond water - cool

Things that happened

Big row broke out on tenniscourt!

Lost child rushing round looking for parents.

Park warden telling off old man about what his dog did.

Movement

tennis players

children rushing about

branches move in breeze

Hearing

sound of tennis game

children shouting

baby crying wind

crunchy gravel path

Smell

mixture of scent from flowers and smell of burger van!

Word pictures

Burger-wrappers blown around like a flock of white birds.

Children chattering like

Brainstorming 2

Use this sheet to fill in ideas and observations of your own. You could fill it in while things are happening – you could brainstorm ideas about your home, or the street where you live for homework. If you are working in school you could use your memories of somewhere such as the supermarket, ice rink or swimming pool, or a really interesting place you have once visited.

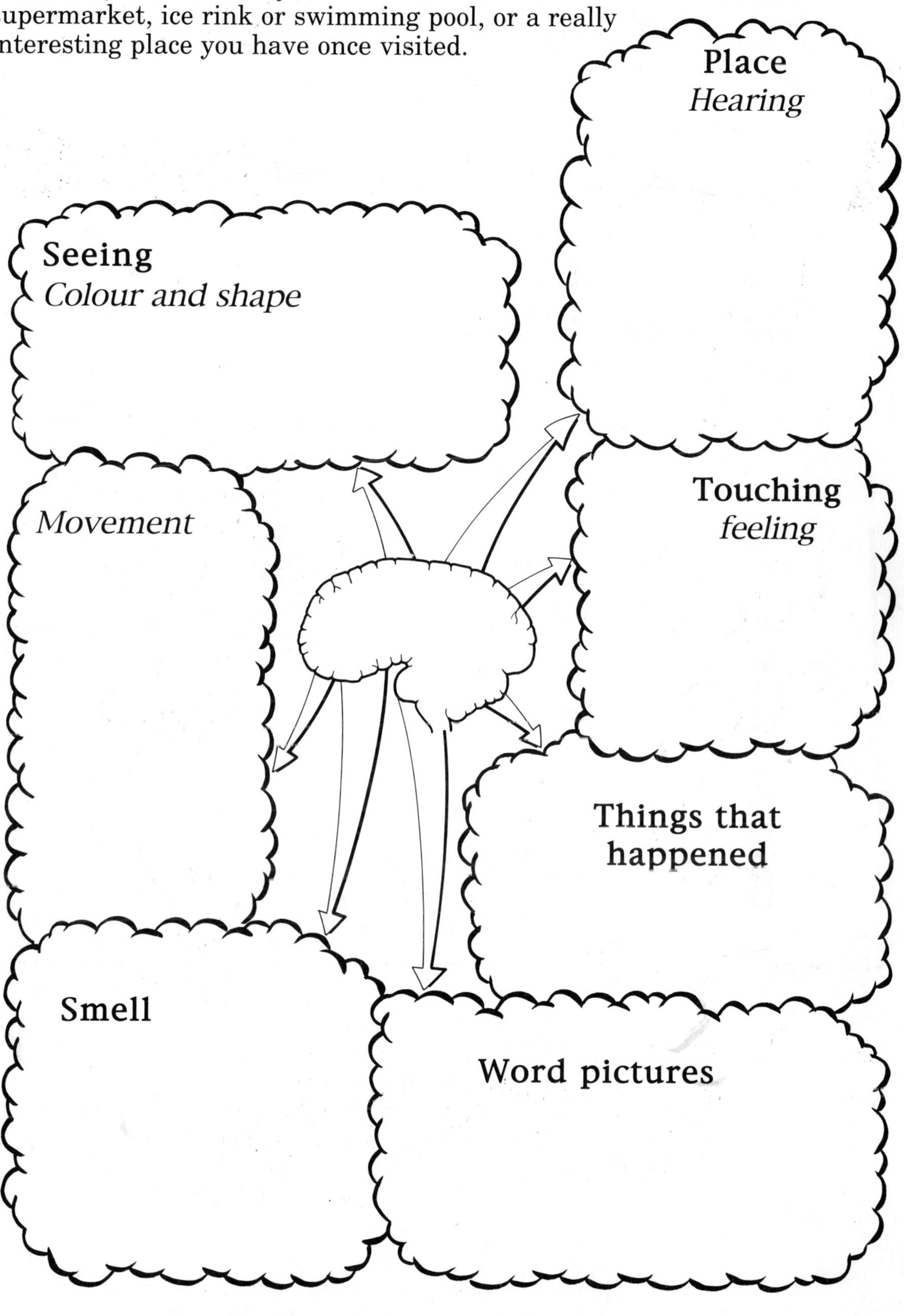

Word pictures

Talk about these very short poems. They describe things by imagining they are something quite different. Use your imagination to finish the 'Washing' poem in the small picture frame, then try to write a 'word picture' of your own in the large picture frame.

November Fog
An elephant sleeps
In the fast lane

March Winds
Cut price postman
brings junk mail
down our street

Snake in the Grass
The hose hisses
Like a poisonous snake
Coiled in the grass

Washing
The white washing
leaping in the wind
Is a

Facts and opinions

Read this extract carefully. It comes from a magazine article. Use different coloured pens to highlight or underline the important information.

- Mark **facts** in one colour.
- Mark **opinions** in another colour.

Electric cars

Many people see the electric car as the transport of the future. They say it will be safer, quieter and non-polluting.

There are many electric vehicles already in use. The most common is the milk float, which for many years has delivered milk to British houses. A new development is the electric bicycle. A battery pack and motor can be attached to an ordinary bicycle to help the rider climb steep hills.

The problem with electric vehicles is really the problem of finding suitable batteries. Batteries are very heavy, they take up a lot of room and need recharging regularly. Electric cars are slow and have a very small range, so they are not much use for long journeys.

Another problem is that they are not really non-polluting. Although they do not give out exhaust fumes they do use electricity which means more pollution from power stations.

Scientists are working hard to solve these problems and maybe the electric car will be a common sight on our roads in the years to come. ■

Pick out six important **facts** about electric vehicles. Write them on the lines below.

1 ______________________________

2 ______________________________

3 ______________________________

4 ______________________________

5 ______________________________

6 ______________________________

Working on notes

Here is a set of lesson notes. The note maker hasn't put the information into good order, and hasn't even said what the notes are about!
Use the information in the notes to write a paragraph about this subject.

Try and put the information into a good order. You do not have to include all the information given. Underline or highlight facts about 'Appearance' in one colour, 'Where they live' in another colour, and 'The way they live' in a third colour.

```
largest - Emperor. 100 cm tall.          live in large flocks
black and white - southern hemisphere - Antarctic          many kinds
Emperor has yellow patches on neck          as far north as equator
    saw some at the zoo once
 not many enemies - leopard seals will catch them
    look like waiters!          can't fly
good swimmers - catch fish with pointed beaks
large webbed feet          King and Emperor - only lay one egg at a time.
```

Listening and note making 1

Work with a partner. Take it in turns to be a reader and a writer.

Are you the reader? Read the information on cobras through carefully to yourself, then read it out to your partner.

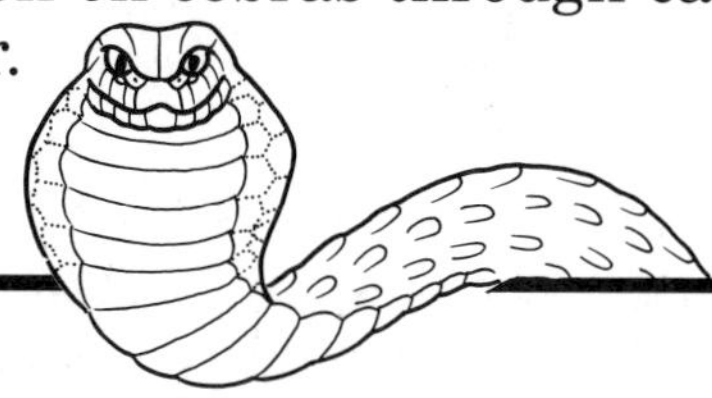

Cobras

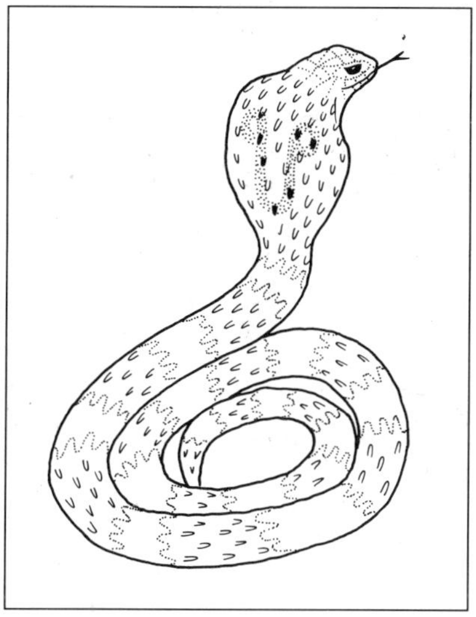

COBRAS are found in hot tropical places, such as Africa and India. When they are angry, they push out their ribs so that the skin behind their heads looks like a hood. There are many types of cobra. They are usually less than two metres long, but the King Cobra can reach three metres.

Cobras lay their eggs in damp places. They feed on small mammals such as mice, and on birds and frogs. They may enter houses in search of food. They are very dangerous animals, for the cobra's bite is one of the most poisonous of all snake bites. A victim might die unless a serum is injected straight away.

Cobras with their fangs removed have been used by 'snake charmers'. The charmers play on musical instruments and the snakes sway to and fro as if they are 'charmed' by the music.

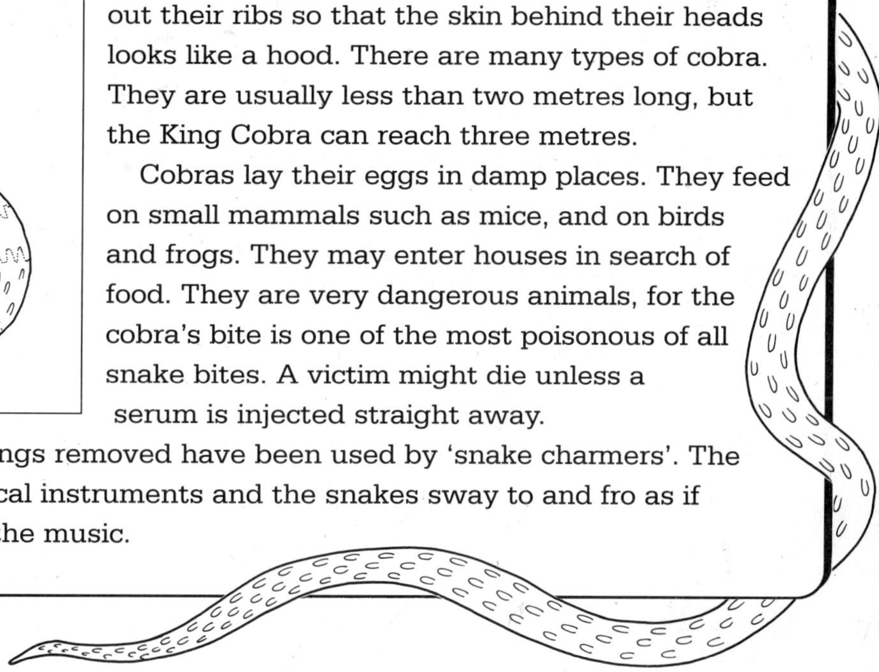

Are you the writer? List the facts you can remember about what your partner has told you. Put them in any order.

Imagine you have to give a talk on this subject. What order would you use for your facts? Put a number in the box to show the order you would use.

Listening and note making 2

Work with a partner. Take it in turns to be a reader and a writer.

Are you the reader? Read the information on kangaroos through carefully to yourself, and then read it out to your partner.

Kangaroos

KANGAROOS are found only in Australia, and nearby islands. There are many kinds, but the best known, the grey kangaroo, is the largest.

A kangaroo has strong back legs and moves by jumping. It can jump as far as eight metres, using its large tail for balance. It eats mainly leaves and twigs, but will also take grain from farmers' fields, jumping over high fences to reach it.

The kangaroo is a pouched mammal. After it is born the tiny baby kangaroo, or 'Joey,' stays in its mother's pouch for about six months. Even after it has learnt to look after itself, it may still return to the pouch when there is danger.

Are you the writer? List the facts you can remember about what your partner has told you. Put them in any order.

______________________________ ☐

______________________________ ☐

______________________________ ☐

______________________________ ☐

______________________________ ☐

______________________________ ☐

______________________________ ☐

______________________________ ☐

Imagine you have to give a talk on this subject. What order would you use for your facts? Put a number in the box to show the order you would use.

Story types

Horror **Western** **Science fiction** **Romance**
Historical **Fantasy** **Ghost stories** **Detective**

Have you read any stories or seen any films from these types?
Write the name of the story or film and its type.

Name ______________________________ Type ______________

You can list other books you have read, or films you have seen, on the back of this sheet.

1

2

3

4

5

6

The time traveller looked at his dial. He gasped. He had arrived in the year 3459! ☐

Roger took Melissa's hand in his... ☐

Hank pushed back his stetson with the barrel of his gun... ☐

But Sir Ponsonby had died between midnight and 2 a.m.... ☐

The coffin creaked open... ☐

Duron the wizard held aloft the great sword of power... ☐

The words and pictures come from some of these story types.
Can you match them?
Choose two of these story types. Write a sentence to say what the story types are about.

______________ stories are about ______________________________

______________ stories are about ______________________________

Story telling – True stories

Work with a partner. Think of a true story – something that has happened to you recently. Here are some ideas:

- a row with your parents
- losing something important, such as a door key
- a time when you looked silly in front of other people
- an incident on a school bus or on a school trip
- a family crisis, such as a flooded kitchen or burnt meal.

Tell your story to your partner. Say what people said, and include lots of detail. Try and make it funny, but not silly.
After listening to the true story, help your partner to fill in the box.

Story report

Story teller ______________________ Listener ______________

Where did the story take place? ______________________

Who was involved? ______________________

What would be a good title for the story? ______________________

Make notes on the main things that happened. The first and last notes have been started for you.

It all started when ______________________

____

____

____

____

____

____

____

____

____

____

____

In the end ______________________

____

____

____

____

Interesting characters 1

Stories and plays need interesting characters!
You can plan out your characters with a character file. Here is a character file of one of the characters in the boxes. Which one do you think it is?

S Jones.

Character file:

Appearance: Short, dark-haired, brown eyes, average build.
Personal history: 14-years-old. Attends Meadowsweet School. Lives with mother and younger brother. Hopes for a career in science.
Special character notes: Always cheerful and friendly, but gets upset when teased about being short. Clever but careless and very untidy. Has many friends. Speaks with a slight Welsh accent.
Stories typical of the character: Once was mistaken for a year 7 pupil by a new teacher. Was given detention for being rude! Once handed in homework covered in paw marks. It had been left on the floor and the dog walked on it!

Plan a character file for a new character. You could choose one of the other characters from the boxes, a real person, or an invented character.

____

Character file:

Appearance: ______________________

Personal history: ______________________

____

Special character notes: ______________________

____

____

____

Stories typical of the character: ______________________

____

____

____

Interesting characters 2

These objects each belong to a different character. Choose one object and invent the character who owns it. Write a character file for your character.

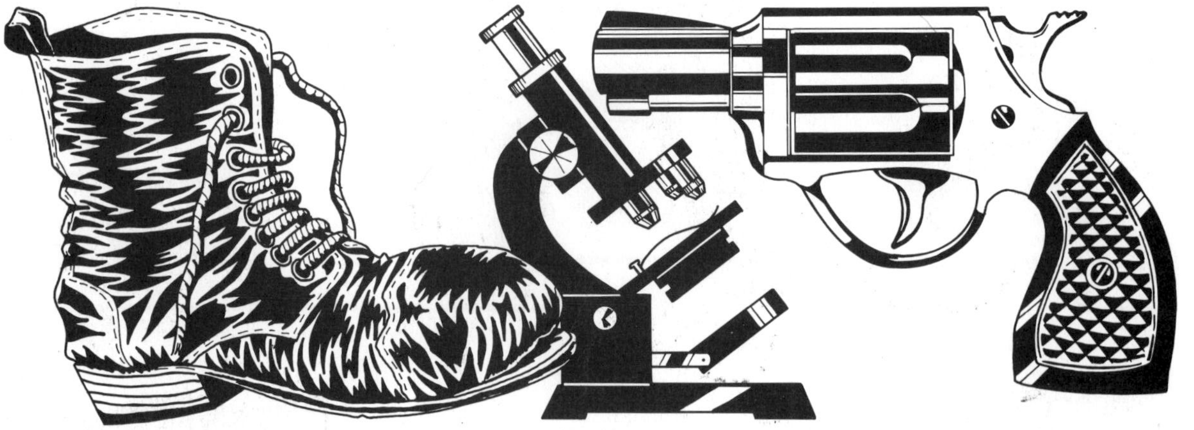

Character file:

Appearance: ____________________

Personal history: ____________________

____

____

Special character notes: ____________________

____

____

____

Stories typical of the character: ____________________

____

____

____

____

Interesting characters 3

Story plots 1 – Climaxes

Read this four-stage story outline. Fill in a happy and a sad ending

1 How it starts

Sarah is wandering down a lonely beach. She sees a cave and thinks she will explore it.

2 A crisis happens

She tries to leave the cave, but the tide has come in and she is trapped!

3 The climax

The water rises higher and higher in the cave. Should she try and swim to safety? She bravely starts swimming through the battering waves…

4 The ending – happy

____

____

____

____

____

or

4 The ending – sad

____

____

____

____

____

Story plots 2 – Confrontations

This story outline uses two characters in conflict.

1 How it starts – character 1

James was sitting back in his chair with his feet on his desk. He was listening to his personal stereo and eating a chocolate bar. He had seen the teacher, Mr Rogers, rushing off in the opposite direction.

2 Character 2 arrives

Mrs Jefferson, the deputy head, walked into the room. James did not notice at first.

3 The confrontation

Mrs Jefferson was furious. She threw the chocolate bar in the bin and confiscated the personal stereo. "You can have it back when you learn to behave like a grown up instead of a six-year-old," she said.

4 The ending – who wins?

That evening, James wrote a letter of apology to Mrs Jefferson. Next day she returned the personal stereo. "What about the chocolate bar?" asked James. Mrs Jefferson glared and James realised he had gone too far...

Use these stages for a story outline of your own. Here are some possible situations:

- policeman and wrong-doer (criminal, speeding motorist, badly behaved teenager)
- parent and son or daughter
- motorist and traffic warden
- two enemies who meet at a party
- neighbours arguing about noise
- trying to get a ball back from a bad-tempered person's garden.

Story-boards 1

These pictures tell a story. Work with a partner to tell the story. One of the pictures is missing – write or draw what happens in the missing part of the story. Make up names for the characters.

The picture on the right comes from a different version of the story. What has happened? Tell the story using this picture. You may need a new ending. Can you think of a way to keep the ending happy?

Story-boards 2

Work with a partner to plan a story using these story-boards. You can use words or pictures. With two sheets you could do both!

1

2

3

4

5

6

In my opinion 1 – Loch Ness Monster

Someone believes in the Loch Ness Monster! She is going to talk about her belief. Here is her planning sheet. She picks out three important pieces of evidence for headings. She thinks about what the people who don't agree might say, and tries to find answers.

Planning sheet

Opinion: I believe the Loch Ness Monster exists!

Reason 1: Many people have reported sightings of the monster.

Reason 2: Photographs of the monster exist.

Reason 3: The loch is very deep and could hide many things.

What others might say:

1 No dead ones have been found.

My answer: The bodies would sink to the bottom of the deep loch.

2 There are no monsters like that in the world.

My answer: There were once! The monster could be a plesiosaur left over from the age of dinosaurs.

Use the blank planning sheet to make notes about your opinion on any subject you feel strongly about – school, home, the law, the environment – or monsters! Here are some other examples – 'I believe eating meat is wrong', 'I believe fox hunting is wrong', 'I believe zoos should be closed down'.

Planning sheet

Opinion:

Reason 1:

Reason 2:

Reason 3:

What others might say:

1

My answer:

2

My answer:

Section 2 Section

Drafting

These sheets provide practice in drafting skills across a range of genres and develop the work done in Section 1. They are designed to develop skills which can be carried over to a student's own writing. The important emphases are: selecting appropriate vocabulary, arranging and structuring notes and first drafts, and looking critically at first attempts.

Drafting can be a teacher intensive activity, particularly when the one to one conference is involved. To overcome this, much use can be made of writing partners and group drafting activities. At the end of the day we are attempting to develop self-criticism in our students; an awareness of the drafting process will enable them to work confidently on their own writing.

Using the worksheets

Paragraphs

Objective: To develop skill in splitting a factual narrative into paragraphs; to introduce the idea of the first sentence being an overview of the paragraph to come.
Students: This sheet can be used by individual students, or by students working in a group for the first part and by themselves for the writing exercise. The writing makes a straightforward homework.
Differentiation: Able students should be able to work through this without prompting. Others will need to discuss the ideas in the information box, and be clear about what is meant by indenting. They should hear the passage read aloud once or twice before starting on the exercise.

Lines of poetry

Objective: To work on lineation in both rhyming and non-rhyming poetry.
Students: This is a good exercise for starting in groups. Discussing why a particular choice has been made can be very valuable.
Differentiation: The teacher may need to expand on the difference between prose and poetry, by reading the examples on the page. The essence of lineation is listening, and an effective reading of these short poems by the teacher will help many students to pick up the idea of listening for the natural pauses.
Notes: 'Lazy Fred' has only one logical line pattern fixed by the rhyme. 'A dog's delight' has rhyme, but there is more than one perfectly valid pattern. The last two poems are unrhymed. 'The White Cat' is fairly easy to sort out, as the commas give the clue. The last poem is much harder. Try to encourage non-rhyming poems for the writing task.

Word choice 1

Objective: To choose appropriate vocabulary in a prose narrative.
Students: This task can be undertaken verbally in a group or as an individual assignment.
Differentiation: The writing task is quite challenging. For less able children a choice of just three or four of the words might be offered, and just a sentence or two asked for.
Notes: The choices are varied. Sometimes there are right/wrong choices, sometimes 'best' choices are asked for. Discussion on why the choice has been made is very valuable.
The original passage is included below.

First day at school
I didn't want to go. Why should I? I could think of no good reason for spoiling what was, after all, a perfectly satisfactory life exactly as it was. I had a friend, I had books, I was fed and watered regularly; why should things change?
Of course I had been past that gate many times; now I had to go through.
"Aren't you lucky?" enthused my mother with a forced smile.
I think she was as nervous as I was.
"Aren't you lucky to go to school today?"
No, I most definitely wasn't!
"I wish I could go to school," continued my mother in desperation.
She took me in. We were greeted cheerfully by the enormous Mrs Mullins, comforting in a blue and black dress which, from my level, seemed to stretch round for ever.
Judith Nicholls

Word choice 2

Objective: A cloze exercise on a poem by Moira Andrew, seeking more imaginative vocabulary.
Students: An appropriate activity for group or pair work. Allow students/groups to compare their ideas after the task has been completed.
Differentiation: The poem could be split up and just one stanza worked on per group. In this case they will still need the whole poem to gain the sense of their stanza. With less able pupils the teacher might write in some of the more difficult missing words, or offer a word bank or even words on a card.
Notes: Try to avoid making this a 'right or wrong' exercise. Let students know that their choices are perfectly valid.
Follow up: Make a composite poem with the class using the best ideas selected by the students. Pick out some of the interesting words thought up by the students and ask for some of them to be used in a piece of writing on a similar subject, that is, night fears. The writing could be prose rather than poetry.
Linked pages: Thesaurus p.30.

Night monster

Monster with teeth, he lives
inside my head until
the moon scribbles its light
across the bedroom walls.

Monster with horns, he sleeps
by day, stirring only when
images of war and famine
cross the television screen.

Monster with spikes, he uncoils,
yawning wide from a great
red throat. He rattles his bars
as I climb the stairs to bed.

Like a chameleon, his colour
changes with each mood. He wears
a tight black skin on a bad night,
grey when he's feeling kind.

He surrounds himself with evil dreams,
but this is no brave monster, so
I stare hard into his yellow eyes,
count to ten and bellow 'Dad!'

Dad stuns him with one blow, shoves
him back behind bars. Together we
print a notice – ***Night monster, please***
do not feed *– and I can sleep safe.*

Moira Andrew

Thesaurus

Objective: To introduce the thesaurus as a means of extending vocabulary.
Students: Individual or group work. The initial work can be done as a class with less confident students.
Notes: A poem is an interesting outcome. A model for the poem might be:

It's just a breeze –
– leaves are gently shaking
It's beginning to gust –
– litter is blowing down the streets
It's becoming a gale –
– ...

This can be written as a class poem, with the teacher providing the model.
Linked pages: Word choice 1 and 2 pp.28 and 29, Word pictures p.6, More word pictures p.33.

In sequence 1

Objective: Sequencing a simple, sequential narrative.
Students: This exercise works well with pairs.
Differentiation: Read the sentences aloud before asking students to start on the exercise. More able students can number the sentences but a better approach is to cut up the sheet and physically rearrange them, perhaps pasting the final choice on to a sheet of paper. The sheet is designed so that this can be done. It would help some students if the first sentence were marked.
Follow up: The 'what happened next' discussion can lead to work on story-boards – see original story below.

Correct sequence

Kevin Potter gunned his small Yamaha down Commercial Road and turned left past the Three Compasses into Gibbet Wharf.

He was bored and fed up because his mates – Chris, Ronnie and Corky – were on holiday.

Kevin had sacrificed his holiday savings to make the first payment on the motorbike.

In a silent patrol car, PCs Edmonds and Kemp heard the bike's exhaust and looked for trouble.

They relaxed as the sound faded into the distance.

Kevin liked riding through the deserted docks at night.

He stopped and looked through a chain-link fence at the railway lines and cranes of the container depot, still floodlit and active.

To the right, the warehouses were just huge shapes in the darkness.

A sudden explosion shattered the night, and tongues of flame shot from the windows of one of the warehouses.

He heard doors slamming, and saw a black Limo accelerating towards him.

Linked pages: Story-boards p.18 and 19.

In sequence 2

Objective: To sequence a set of instructions.
Students: Individuals or pairs.
Differentiation: The picture clues will help a good deal. For pupils requiring a greater challenge the pictures could be removed. For less able students, talk through the recipe in a general way before starting them off on the exercise.
Notes: This is another sequential text but not as obviously sequential as the story.
Follow up: Ask students to write out a recipe of their own in such a way that it can be cut up. Pass the cut up recipes to another student to arrange. An amusing game is to mix up two recipes – say chocolate pudding and cheese and tomato pizza – and ask students to sort them out before ordering them. It would help to have some recipes ready, perhaps on a computer.
Linked pages: The completed recipes can be used for Working on a script p.39.

More word pictures

Objective: To make 'bald and unconvincing' narratives into more interesting ones by developing the vocabulary and imagery.
Instructions: Read and talk about the worked example first. Read the second passage aloud, and talk about possible words that might be included in a piece of writing on: 'A sunny beach'.
Students: The writing task can be done individually or in pairs, or scribed by a support teacher.
Differentiation: Provide a word bank in advance for less able students, but insist that they add some words of their own to it.
Linked pages: Word pictures p.6, Poetry 1 and 2 pp.52 and 53.

Redrafting 1

Stories

Objective: To develop critical skills, and drafting skills for story writing.
Students: Talking and discussion as a class or in groups; writing individually or in pairs.
Differentiation: The writing task can be done by the teacher scribing ideas from a group.
Linked pages: Story plots 1 – Climaxes p.16, Punctuation 4 – "and" p.122.

Redrafting 2

Prose

Objective: To look critically at a piece of factual prose writing.
Students: This task works best in groups, with a secretary to write down the conclusions of the group discussion.
Notes: The text has organisational weaknesses, and requires discussion on a more effective sequencing of the information. The second task requires some thinking about artwork, organisation of a project, and so on.
Follow up: Ask more able students to rewrite the passage. They will need to list main points and rearrange them in a more effective order. Less able students could highlight the main points.
Linked pages: Facts and opinions p.7, Working on notes p.8.

Redrafting 3
Poetry

Objective: To work on the redrafting of a poem.
Students: Discussion with a class or within a group. Writing by groups or by a class, or with teacher/support teacher scribing.
Notes: The areas covered in the drafting work are vocabulary building, developing images, and lineation. The 'Questions to ask' box can be used by students to help them with their own poetry writing.
Linked pages: Word pictures p.6, More word pictures p.33, Lines of poetry p.27, Word choice 2 p.29, Thesaurus p.30.

Mini-stories

Objective: Detailed editing work on a very short narrative.
Students: Individual or pair work.
Notes: The object of the mini-story is to produce a complete story in exactly 50 words. To achieve this students will need to look at each word in turn, cut out all redundancies and rewrite to make phrases shorter and clearer.

(In the detective story, the surviving twin is guilty because he switched identity before killing his twin brother to wipe out his own debts. We know this because the dead twin is a heavy smoker (stained fingers!) while the surviving twin is playing the part of his smoking brother, but not successfully because he is spluttering and tears are running down his cheeks – he is not used to smoking!)

Differentiation: Less able pupils might aim at slightly longer stories, and be given a margin of between 90 and 100 words. Counting words is a good exercise.
Linked pages: Redrafting 1 – Stories p.34.

Script conference

Objective: A co-operative exercise in planning.
Students: Work in groups of three or four.
Notes: Ensure students understand 'setting'.
Differentiation: This exercise can work well in a small group with a support teacher acting as secretary. The outcome can be a written script, or an improvised play.
Linked pages: Make use of these pages to help with developing ideas: Interesting characters 2 p.14, Story plots 1 – Climaxes p.16, Story plots 2 – Confrontations p.17, Storyboards 2 p.19. Playscript 1 p.56 gives help on setting out a script.

Working on a script

Objective: To give practice in scriptwriting, script conferencing, improvisation.
Students: Work in groups of three or four.
Differentiation: A support teacher can act as scribe. Have possible recipes available. Locations could be written on cards. Some students will be helped by suggestions for locations (club, school, alien planet, the school bus) and characters (aliens, teacher, policeman, other 'authority' figures, themselves).
Follow up: Work towards a tape version of the cookery show.
Linked pages: Script conference p.38, Playscript 1 p.56, In sequence 2 p.32.

Paragraphs

A **paragraph** is a group of sentences in a piece of writing. The sentences cover one topic. When the topic changes, we start a new paragraph. The first sentence is often used to introduce the paragraph.

In a story, we start a new paragraph when there is a change in the action of the story. How many paragraphs are in this box? How can you tell?

Read this account of Hayley Malone. It should have been divided into three paragraphs. Decide where the new paragraphs should start. Put a slash sign (/) where you want to start the paragraphs and write 'para' in the margin.

Hayley Malone – superstar

Hayley Malone was born in 1974 in Southend, Essex. She did not find school work easy but she was always popular with her friends. She loved dressing up, singing and dancing, and was always involved in school concerts and plays. Her first big break came in 1991 when she auditioned for a part in the popular TV soap *West End Street*. She played the part of Donna Durrant, a rebellious young teenager. She became hugely popular, and soon she found herself in great demand for all sorts of events. She opened supermarkets, made appearances on chat shows, and was interviewed by fan magazines. By 1995 she was tired of the hard work involved in being a soap star and launched her new career as a pop singer with her first single 'Little Lost Girl'. Sadly, Hayley's singing career was not a success. Although thousands of pounds were poured into publicity, people soon realised that there was a problem. Hayley couldn't sing!

Write three paragraphs about yourself. You can use these paragraph starters, or think of your own.

I was born…
One of the highlights of my life has been…
I came to this school in…
One of my worst accidents was when…
One day I would like…

Continue over the page.

Lines of poetry

A story, or an account of something, is written in **prose**. When we write prose, we don't start a new line until we get to the edge of the page, or until we want to start a new paragraph.

Poems can be written with lines of any length. Sometimes, we end lines with a rhyme. In a non-rhyming poem, a new line can help the reader to see where there is a pause. This makes it easier to read the poem aloud.

The poems on this page have not been divided into lines. Talk about them, and decide where to start the new lines. Use a slash (/) to mark the new lines. (Reading the poems aloud is the best way to 'hear' where the lines should start.)

Here lie the bones of
lazy Fred who
wasted precious
time in bed some
plaster fell down on
his head and thanks
be praised our
Freddie's dead.

It's a dog's delight to bark
and bite and little birds to
sing, and if you sit on a red
hot brick it's a sign of an
early spring.

The white cat stood on three legs, tested
the snow with its fourth, sniffed the air,
flicked a disapproving tail, and returned to
its snug bed by the fire.

Trees come to life in your imagination, and
a giant holding his breath under water
has his hair peeping out – bulrushes for
birds to nest in.

Write a short descriptive poem of your own using only four or five lines. Think carefully about where your lines end.

Word choice 1

Read this passage. Judith Nicholls is describing her first day at school. Make the best choice of the words in the brackets. Cross out the words you don't want.

First day at school

I didn't want to go. Why should I? I could think of no good (method/reason/use) for spoiling what was, after all, a perfectly (good/satisfactory/boring) life exactly as it was. I had a friend, I had books, I was fed and watered regularly; why should things change? (On/off/of) course I had been past that gate many (days/mornings/times); now I had to go (through/in/on).

"Aren't you lucky?" (argued/enthused/said) my mother with a forced smile.

I think she was as nervous as I was.

"Aren't you (old enough/lucky/happy) to go to school today?"

No, I most definitely wasn't!

"I wish I (could go/had been) to school," continued my mother in (anger/desperation/fun).

She took me in. We were greeted (gratefully/first/cheerfully) by the enormous Mrs Mullins, (pretty/comforting/dazzling) in a blue and black dress which, from my (level/way/angle), seemed to stretch round for ever.

Judith Nicholls

Here are some words from the rest of the story. Choose some of them to continue the story in your own words.

child, pictures, knee, desks, playtime, boys, alphabet, infants, unwilling, juniors, wave, bigger, classroom, cried, home

The words in the box below do not come from the story, but you can use them in your version if you wish.

howled	glared	enormous	tough	scruffy	thump

Word choice 2

This poem by Moira Andrew has some of its words and phrases missing. Choose words to fill the gaps. You can choose more than one for each.

Although Moira Andrew has made her own word choices, this does not mean that her words are right and yours are wrong. When you have worked on the poem, compare your word choices with the choices of others. Your teacher has a copy of the original poem which you might like to look at.

Night monster

Monster with teeth, he lives
inside my ________________ until
the moon ________________ its light
across the bedroom walls.

Monster with ________________, he sleeps
by day, stirring only when
images of ________________ and famine
cross the television screen.

Monster with ________________, he ________________,
yawning wide from a great
red ________________. He rattles his bars
as I climb the stairs to bed.

Like a ________________, his colour
changes with each mood. He wears
a ________________ skin on a bad night,
grey when he's feeling ________________.

He surrounds himself with ________________,
but this is no brave monster, so
I ________________ into his ________________ eyes,
count to ten and bellow 'Dad!'

Dad ________________ him with one blow, shoves
him ________________. Together we
print a notice – **Night monster, please
do not** ________________ – and I can sleep safe.

Moira Andrew

Thesaurus

A **thesaurus** is a special type of dictionary. Words are not in alphabetical order. They are arranged in groups according to their meaning.

If you look up a word like 'hot', you will find a list of words such as scorching, red hot, boiling, toasting, and sweltering.

A thesaurus is very useful as it offers you a wide choice of words for your writing.

Make your own thesaurus.
How many words similar in meaning to 'excellent' can you think of?
Write them down here.

excellent ____________________

Now see how many words similar to 'excellent' you can find in the thesaurus. A thesaurus also gives you lists of types.

Add as many words as you can to this list.

burglar **pickpocket** **thief** **pirate**

The words in the box below were found in a thesaurus under 'windy'. Use some of them in a story or poem about a day that is getting windier and windier!

breeze	moderate wind	gust	blast	blow
flurry	gale	storm	squall	

In sequence 1

These sentences come from the beginning of a story called 'Burn-up'. Put them in the best order, then paragraph them.

They relaxed as the sound faded into the distance.

To the right, the warehouses were just huge shapes in the darkness.

He heard doors slamming, and saw a black Limo accelerating towards him.

Kevin had sacrificed his holiday savings to make the first payment on the motorbike.

In a silent patrol car, PCs Edmonds and Kemp heard the bike's exhaust and looked for trouble.

He was bored and fed up because his mates – Chris, Ronnie and Corky – were on holiday.

A sudden explosion shattered the night, and tongues of flame shot from the windows of one of the warehouses.

Kevin liked riding through the deserted docks at night.

He stopped and looked through a chain-link fence at the railway lines and cranes of the container depot, still floodlit and active.

Kevin Potter gunned his small Yamaha down Commercial Road and turned left past the Three Compasses into Gibbet Wharf.

Talk about what happens next. How many ways can you think of to complete the story?

In sequence 2

This recipe for cottage pie is very muddled! Cut out the instructions and arrange them in a more sensible order. The pictures will help you.

Spread the potatoes over the mince.

Fry the onion until it is soft.

Tip the cooked mince into a glass dish.

Fry the mince until it is cooked (about 15 minutes) adding water and cornflower to thicken.

Put some oil in a frying pan and add the onion, crushed garlic and paprika.

Bake in a hot oven until the potatoes are nicely browned.

Peel and cut up the potatoes, then boil in salted water.

Add the mince, the stock cube, and a pinch of salt.

You will need:
500 grams minced meat (beef or lamb)
1 onion
1 stock cube
1 clove of fresh garlic, or half a teaspoon of garlic powder
1 teaspoon of paprika
cornflower
750 grams of potatoes
salt and pepper
butter if wanted

When the potatoes are cooked, drain and mash. Add butter if required.

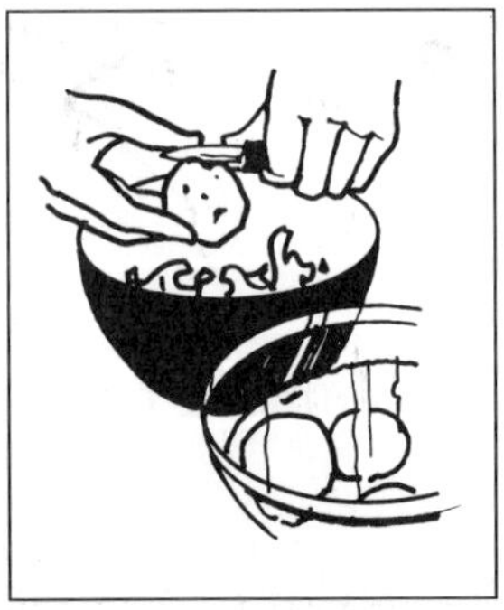

More word pictures

Adding word pictures can make a dull piece of writing interesting!

Version A

Christmas shopping was in full swing. Shoppers rushed into the shops and the most popular counters were really busy. The windows were lit up and Christmas tree lights flashed on and off. Everywhere could be heard the sound of people's feet as they went round spending their money.

Homeless people were begging in doorways.

Version B

Christmas shopping was in full swing. Shoppers rushed madly into this shop and that as if this was the last chance for shopping in their whole lives, and the most popular counters heaved like football matches. Windows blazed and Christmas trees winked like drunk uncles. Everywhere could be heard the tramp, tramp of tired boots on wet pavements. Money burned holes in pockets, bounced, and rattled into cash registers.

Meanwhile, huddled for warmth in dark doorways of empty shops, the homeless stretched out empty hands.

Talk about what makes Version B more interesting. You will need to think about describing words (adjectives and adverbs) and about word pictures or comparisons.

Now work on this passage. Talk about words that might be useful. Brainstorm for the word bank before you start.

The sun was hot. The sandy beach stretched right round the bay. The sea was blue. The beach was crowded with people. They had coloured beach umbrellas. The people were sunbathing and were very brown. Children splashed about a lot in the water. Out at sea an oil slick came nearer.

Word bank

Redrafting 1 - Stories

Read this extract from the first draft of a story by Wendy.

Cliff rescue

Tanya lowered the rope over the edge of the cliff. David was worried that it might fray on a sharp stone and break when they were pulling Ghita up. He put a coat on the edge. Tanya shouted down to Ghita on the ledge "Sit in the loop when it comes down. Shout when you're ready and we'll haul you up". Soon Ghita was safe.

Wendy talked about the extract with her writing partners. They thought that it wasn't exciting or interesting enough yet. Wendy agreed!

Talk about the extract, and decide how it could be made more interesting and exciting. Work on a second draft of Wendy's story.

Redrafting 2 - Prose

Here is the introduction of a project on the guitar by Sean. Make a list of the important facts. Put them in good order.

> The modern guitar was invented in the 19th century in Spain. Before that there were instruments quite like it. The guitar had seven strings in the 17th century but in the 19th century this became six. Some strings used to be made of animal guts and the deep ones of metal covered with silk. The instrument is played by plucking the strings. Chords can be played by playing some of the strings together. Nowadays some of the strings are metal and some are made of plastic. The guitar is used for all sorts of music, such as pop music, classical music, and jazz. For pop music an electric guitar is used. This needs an amplifier. There are many designs of electric guitar.

Now answer these questions.

How could Sean improve his project introduction?

____

____

____

____

____

____

____

____

What else does this project need to make it really interesting? How could this be done?

____

____

____

____

____

____

____

____

Redrafting 3 - Poetry

Read the first draft of Richard's poem, printed below.

Questions to ask when you are drafting a poem

Is the choice of words interesting?
Are there any words that can be cut out to improve the poem?
Has the poet used any interesting word pictures?
Has the poem got a good ending?
Are the line endings in the right place?
Does the poem use punctuation well?
Does it sound good when it is read out?

Wolf – draft one

A wolf is a grey cloud
It storms down on its prey
Like lightning and thunder it
Starts to kill the animal.
The boom, it dies.
The wolf creeps off,
The thunder dies down,
All has gone, until another day.

He talked about it with a writing partner and with his teacher, then thought about what should happen next.

Here is Richard's second draft.

Wolf – draft two

A wolf is a grey cloud.
It storms down on its prey
Like lightning and thunder.
He starts to kill his victim.
Boom! The animal dies
The wolf eats then
Creeps off
The thunder dies down.
All has gone, until another day.

Talk about the changes Richard has made in his poem. Is the poem improved?

Richard was still not happy with his poem. Work together on a third version. Use the drafting suggestions in the box above to help you.

Mini-stories

The detective examined the body. A hole in the head dripped blood. A revolver lay by his stained fingers.

The victim's identical twin smoked nervously. Tears ran down his face. "He was in serious debt," he spluttered. "He killed himself!"

"He didn't!" said the detective. "I arrest you for murder!"

This story has [ ] words.

How did the detective solve the crime?

Count the number of words. Put the number in the box. Mini-stories have *exactly* this number of words. The mini-story below has too many words. Work through it and make it the right number. You will have to change words and sentences as well as just cutting out words.

It was a cold, snowy night in December. The family heard a knock at the door. Father opened it.

"Aunt Edith!" he said, surprised. "What are you doing here? And where is your coat? You must be freezing!"

Saying nothing, Aunt Edith stretched out her hands to the fire, then disappeared!

The phone rang.

"Sorry to tell you, Sir, but your Aunt's body has just been found. She froze to death two days ago..."

Try your own mini-stories. Write a first draft without worrying about the length, then try and cut it down to the right number of words.

Script conference

Television plays and series are often planned at a **script conference**. A team of writers will decide on important matters like the characters, settings (places where the action happens), and the story line before the script is written.

TV plays often have a tight budget. This means that there can't be too many characters, or too many changes of scene.

Set up your script conference now. You will need a chairperson to organise the conference, and a secretary to make notes. Work together on the summary below.

Budget: your budget is very limited! You are allowed:

3 characters

____

____

____

2 settings

____

____

Your play should not last for more than five minutes.

Summary of what was decided. Think about the beginning, middle and end of your play.

____

____

____

____

____

____

____

____

____

____

____

Working on a script

Here is a short extract from a script from *Cook it with Crockett*, a cookery show hosted by crazy cook Barry Crockett.

LOCATION: SERVICE STATION CAR PARK ON THE M6 MOTORWAY.
CARS, TRUCKS THUNDERING PAST.
CUT TO BARRY BEHIND TABLE WITH COOKER, INGREDIENTS.
A CROWD OF PEOPLE LOOK ON.

BARRY Welcome to the M6! Here we have a merry crowd of motorists, fed up with being ripped off in expensive motorway cafés. I'm going to cook a special dish called lamb chops with cones, à la M6! It's tasty, it's good for you, and it won't break the bank! But first a swig of this most delicious lemonade! (BARRY DRINKS)

Now lets have a look at the ingredients. First, some chopped onions. I'll chuck them in the pan in a minute and get them sizzling...

Now you have an idea of Barry's style, work on the script for next week's show. Before you start, you will need to decide:

- What Barry is going to cook (keep it simple).
  Suggestions: pizza, cottage pie, fish and chips, or something more unusual – mixed jelly or birds nest soup... or anything else whacky you can think of!

- What interesting location you are going to use.

Try improvising Barry's speech in groups. Write down the best ideas and use them in your script.

Section 3 Section

Writing forms

This section looks at the many forms and genres of writing: narrative, poetry, playscript, letters, reportage, descriptive and persuasive writing, informal writing, biography and autobiography. The individual worksheets provide frameworks for writing, getting over the difficult business of getting started. The aim of the section as a whole is to show the various functions and purposes of writing, from the practical to the imaginative. Students should be encouraged to consider a range of strategies for writing narratives and writing about their own experiences. A series of letters or diary entries might make an unusual approach to a story; a playscript might serve as a new way of looking at an historical event or character.

Using the worksheets

Direct speech

Objective: To provide starters for writing a conversation in direct speech.
Students: Individual or pair work.
Differentiation: The initial exercise can be worked through as a class, and the conversation improvised before the writing stage.
Linked pages: If students are unsure of the techniques of setting out direct speech they should work through Punctuation 4 – "and" p.122.

Indirect speech

Objective: To introduce indirect speech through reportage.
Students: Pairs or individual writing.
Differentiation: Less able pupils may need further explanation, with examples, of the details in the information box. Improvise the interviews with Gary Collins and Billy Rottweiller to bring out the difference between what they actually said and what is reported in the article. The chosen headline could also be improvised before writing starts.
Linked pages: Reportage 1 – Reporter's notebook p.65, Reportage 2 – Sports report p.66.

Story 1 – The missing section

Objective: More work on structuring stories.
Students: This is best started as class or group discussion.
Notes: Photocopy the story, covering over one the three sections. Discuss what happens in the missing section before setting the writing task. For a more able group, hand out a mixture of versions – some missing the first section, some the second, some the last. Make up a story entirely from the sections written by the students.
Follow up: Try the same exercise, using stories written by the students.
Linked pages: Story 2 – Beginning, middle and end p.51, Story plots 1 – Climaxes p.16, Story-boards 2 p.19.

Story 2 – Beginning, middle and end

Objective: Further work on story structure emphasising beginnings, middles and ends.
Students: Individuals, pairs or groups.
Differentiation: The sentences can be cut up and physically rearranged if preferred.
Follow up: The two stories can be expanded, either as a written exercise or in discussion. Use the various planning and drafting exercises detailed below to help build up the stories, particularly story-boards.
Linked pages: Story plots 1 – Climaxes p.16, Story-boards 2 p.19, Redrafting 1 – Stories p.34, Interesting characters 1–3 pp.13–15.

Poetry 1 – What am I?

Objective: To carry forward the student's understanding of simile and metaphor introduced in Word pictures p.6 and More word pictures p.33.
Students: Group or pair work enables students to pool ideas and build up the list as a team.
Notes: The words simile and metaphor are not introduced in these materials, the words 'word pictures' or 'comparisons' being simpler. The

teacher may wish to introduce the technical terms, but knowledge of the distinctions between simile, metaphor and personification is less important than understanding what they do, i.e. they offer an imaginative comparison. This worksheet offers a pattern for building riddles, by personifying, or 'bringing to life' inanimate objects or ideas. The riddle answers are: sea, rain, tree, bridge.
Differentiation/extension: Try working on abstract ideas such as 'I am anger' or 'I am greed'.
Linked pages: Word pictures p.6, More word pictures p.33, Poetry 2 – Two-line poems p.53.

POETRY 2 – TWO-LINE POEMS

Objective: Further work on imaginative comparisons, providing a simple structure for writing.
Students: This is effective as pair work, as explained on the sheet.
Notes: This pattern is based on the poem 'In the station of the metro' by Ezra Pound. The first line presents the real world (A crisp bag swirling through the air) and the second the imaginative comparison (an alien space ship sucked into a black hole). The two lines are linked by a semi-colon that allows a suitable 'pause for reflection'.
Differentiation: If the concept is difficult to grasp, work with the class on one of the first lines on the sheet, talking through the idea and building up a 'list poem' of alternative ideas.
Linked sheets: Word pictures p.6, More word pictures p.33, Poetry 1 – What am I? p.52, Punctuation 3 – Semi-colons, colons and dashes p.121.

POETRY 3 – SYLLABLES

Objective: To introduce/reinforce the concept of syllables.
Students: The list-filling exercise can be done individually or through class/group discussion. The haiku writing is an individual task.
Notes: The object of the exercise is to gain a feel for syllables, an important part of auditory discrimination. Use redrafting (Redrafting 3 – Poetry p.36) and look at alternative words (Thesaurus p.30) to find the correct number of syllables. The haiku given here contain similes. This is not a requirement of the form, but it offers a simple pattern. Students can use the two-line poems (Poetry 2) to turn into haiku.
Differentiation: There is no simple and easily understood definition of a syllable, and it is best explained by example. If students are still struggling with the idea of a syllable, work on their own given names, John, Naresh, Catherine, Victoria, and count the syllables. Regional accents often introduce extra syllables into words – the intrusive 'y' turning whale into 'way-ull', for example. The teacher will need to decide whether it is appropriate to accept this.
Linked pages: Poetry 2 – Two-line poems p.53, Redrafting 3 – Poetry p.36, Thesaurus p.30.

POETRY 4 – I AM

Objective: To offer a simple structure for a poem based on the idea of a persona, or first person narrative. Students 'become' the object.
Students: This is a straightforward individual exercise, following discussion and explanation.
Differentiation: Some pupils may need help with thinking up a suitable object. Pictures of scrap yards, ruined houses, etc, may provide the spark.
Linked pages: First person – Using 'I' p.108.

PLAYSCRIPT 1

Objective: To introduce the special format of a playscript.
Students: Work together on the rules of playscript writing. The continuation can be a group or individual effort following discussion/improvisation.
Notes: It is standard form for broadcast scripts to use the 'everything in capitals bar the words spoken' rule. School play texts do not always adhere to this rule. Some students do not find capital letters easy to read or write, and you may wish to compromise on this aspect of script writing.
Linked pages: Playscript 2 p.57, Script conference p.38, Working on a Script p.39.

Playscript 2

Objective: An exercise in redrafting direct and indirect speech into playscript.
Students: Groups should be offered the chance to work on the extract of their choice.
Notes: Use the Script conference (p.38) structure to help develop the play. Encourage groups to improvise, particularly in *Caught Red Handed* which is in indirect speech.
Differentiation: The teacher may wish to read through the extracts a couple of times before the groups start work on the scripts. Ask the students to highlight the spoken words. A teacher or support teacher can act as a scribe.
Follow up: The scripts can be photocopied and performed.
Linked pages: Playscript 1 p.56, Script conference p.38, Working on a Script p.39.

Diary 1 – Long and short

Objective: To look at first person writing using the diary form; expanding notes to make a continuous narrative.
Students: Individual or pair work.
Notes: Talk through how the second extract expands on the first by including feelings and responses to the incidents, including humorous comment. Talk about how the character of Aunt Jean might be brought to life.
Differentiation: The teacher can act as scribe, collecting ideas from a group.
Linked pages: Story telling – True stories p.12, Autobiography 2 p.81, Diary 2 – Making it interesting p.59, Redrafting 1 – Stories p.34, Personal writing p.88, First person – Using 'I' p.108.

Diary 2 – Making it interesting

Objective: Diary writing based on real experience.
Students: Individual work.
Notes: Use the idea of expanding work done in Diary 1 – Long and short (p.58). It is important to point out that the final piece of work should not include details of every hour of the day. The writer should pick out the most interesting notes to expand, and discard the rest.
Differentiation: Students can work with a partner or support teacher acting as scribe. An alternative method is to cut up the phrases in the short diary, leaving room for more detail to be written in. Another possibility is to save the short diary text on a computer, asking the students (in groups) to expand it.
Linked pages: Diary 1 – Long and short p.58, Story telling – True stories p.12, Autobiography 2 – I'm the sort of person that… p.81, Redrafting 1 – Stories p.34, Personal writing p.88, First person – Using 'I' p.108.

Letters and envelopes

Objective: Practical information and practice in setting out letters and envelopes correctly.
Students: Talk through the information with the class, then set the tasks as individual work.
Linked pages: Letters 1, 2 and 3 pp.61-3.

Letters 1 – Setting it out

Objective: To work on formal letters.
Students: Choices can be the result of pair or group discussion.
Differentiation: The whole exercise can be done as a class, with the teacher entering the results, or, the options can be reduced by being blanked out before the page is copied.
Follow up: Other letters in list A can be written as individual written work.
Linked pages: Letters and envelopes p.60, Letters 2 and 3 pp.62-3.

Letters 2 – Getting that job

Objective: To work on a job application letter.
Students: Class work to begin with, then individual writing.
Notes: The letter is taken from 'In Reply to your Advertisement', by John Kirkbride, published by Scholastic Publications Ltd 1989. The teacher should read the letter out, emphasising the laid back humour of the writer. Suggest that students underline or highlight particularly inappropriate phrases.

The letter is substantial and so it is not proposed that students work on a redraft of this.
Linked pages: Letters and envelopes p.60, Letters 1 – Setting it out p.61.

Letters 3 – Complaining

Objective: Writing a letter of complaint, based on the information provided on the sheet.
Students: Individual or paired writing.
Notes: Suggest students make a list of complaints and work them into a draft letter before starting on the final letter.
Extension: If there is a local contentious issue of sufficient interest, use the same approach to write a letter to the local paper.
Linked pages: Working on notes p.8, Letters and envelopes p.60, Letters 1 – Setting it out p.61.

Speech bubbles

Objective: Matching dialogue to a strip cartoon using speech bubbles.
Students: Individual or group work.
Notes: Students can write the words or the appropriate letter in the speech bubbles. (Or cut off the text and allow students to choose their own words for the bubbles).
Follow up: A page from a comic can be copied (with permission) with the bubbles blanked out.

Reportage 1 Reporter's notebook

Objective: Writing newspaper reports.
Students: Discussion on the reports as a class, writing in pairs.
Notes: Ensure students are familiar with the indirect speech worksheet before tackling this exercise.
Linked pages: Indirect speech p.49, Working on notes p.8.

Reportage 2 – Sports report

Objective: To look closely at a report of a sports event.
Students: Read and talk about the report as a class. The writing task can be done in pairs, one acting as reporter and the other as a sub editor, as in Reportage 1 – Reporter's notebook.
Differentiation: The number of elements make this quite a difficult task. The page could be simplified by blanking out some of the bulletted (■) elements.
Linked pages: Reportage 1 – Reporter's notebook p.65, Indirect speech p.49, Working on notes p.8.

Describing places 1 – Planning it out

Objective: To produce well thought out accounts of places the students have visited.
Students: Individual or group work. The writing task could be individual or pair work, or scribed by a partner/support teacher.
Notes: Read the extract aloud and talk through the bulletted points. Emphasise the note making stage of the writing activity. If possible, talk through these notes and the 'first sentences' before the remainder of the writing is undertaken.
Linked pages: Describing places 2 – Good and bad p.68, Working on notes p.8, Listening and note making 1 and 2 pp.9 and 10.

Describing places 2 – Good and bad

Objective: Further work on describing places, emphasising the student's opinion of the place described. An exercise in building sustained writing from notes.
Students: The introductory material should be worked on by the whole class or group. The 'good points and bad points' could be prepared in pairs, with the final accounts written individually.
Notes: Insist on a balanced point of view about the place, particularly if 'school' is chosen.
Differentiation: The writing task could be a whole class/group effort, with the teacher/support teacher assembling the notes in the first instance.
Linked pages: Describing places 1 – Planning it out p.67, Working on notes p.8, Listening and note making 1 and 2 pp.9 and 10.

Instructions 1 – Cassette recorder

Objective: To produce a set of operating instructions for a cassette recorder.
Students: Individual or group work.
Notes: Ensure that all students are familiar with operating cassette recorders. Most record/playback devices – personal stereos, CD players, videos – have the same basic layout, although some require two buttons to be pressed for the 'record' function. The students should aim at a logical sequence in their instructions, and it is worth talking this through. Should 'play' or 'record' come first?
Differentiation: Some students may like to record their instructions on to tape. They will, of course, be unable to do this unless they can understand their own instructions!
Linked pages: In sequence 2 p.32, Working on notes p.8, Second person – Hey, you! p.109.

Instructions 2 – Feeding the pet

Objective: To produce an imaginary set of instructions in the form of a letter.
Students: Individual work.
Notes: Encourage students to make their instructions as funny as possible!
Linked pages: Letters 3 – Complaining p.63, Instructions 1 – Cassette recorder p.69, Second person – Hey, you! p.109.

Providing information 1 – Fire!

Objective: Simplifying language for a set of instructions.
Students: This works well as a group exercise.
Notes: Ensure that the students themselves fully understand the instructions before they start simplifying. Ask them to think about difficult words, and breaking up long sentences into short ones. Students may like to discuss whether pictures would help to explain the words.
Differentiation: If students find the task of simplifying too difficult, they may find it easier to write a simple set of instructions for their own classroom.
Linked pages: Instructions 1 – Cassette recorder p.69, Thesaurus p.30, Second person – Hey, you! p.109.

Providing information 2 – Welcome to our school!

Objective: To produce a mini-brochure for the school.
Students: A group exercise.
Notes: The sheet should be folded so that both sides are used. Extra sheets can be stapled inside for a more substantial project. The 'front' of the brochure should have the school name and perhaps a logo or picture.
Differentiation: Students with a feel for computer work may like to redesign the layout on the computer and desk top publish the entire brochure.
Extension: Use a similar design for writing about a club or activity.
Linked pages: Headings p.128, Desk top publishing p.132, Questionnaire p.79, Describing places 2 – Good and bad p.68.

Providing information 3 – Packaging

Objective: To design packaging for a product.
Students: An individual, paired or group task.
Notes: Talk through the tick options with the group. Some products will require only some of these. Ask which options are to be found on all products. The students will need to create a name for their product. A group discussion would be a good way to develop the product.
Extension: Further written work could be done on advertising and marketing the new product.
Linked pages: Desk top publishing p.132, Headings p.128, Persuasion 1 p.74.

Persuasion 1 – Advertising

Objective: To work on honest and dishonest advertising, and to prepare an advertisement according to the rules.

Students: Talking in groups or as a class. The new advertisement can be planned as a group exercise or designed by individuals.
Notes: Look at a selection of real advertisements to see how they persuade before starting the exercise.
Linked pages: Desk top publishing p.132, Providing information 3 – Packaging p.73.

Persuasion 2 – Junk food

Objective: Working on a piece of persuasive writing on an issue of interest to the students; looking closely at the structure of the writing.
Students: Class discussion followed by individual writing.
Notes: Discuss the point of view in the passage, looking for further arguments. The three-part structure to the writing is quite a difficult concept and help will be needed with this. Ask students to highlight the three parts. Point out that in the passage each part has a paragraph of its own. Encourage an ideas brainstorm using 'for and against' as headings. Use the 'In my opinion' planning sheet to pick out the important ideas.
Differentiation: For most students it is best to read the passage aloud, then ask them to read it silently to themselves. The 'clincher' is a difficult idea and this will need to be talked through.
Linked pages: In my opinion 1 p.20, Paragraphs p.26, Speech writing p.77.

Persuasion 3 – Small ads

Objective: To look at and write small ads; to use editing and abbreviating skills.
Students: Group discussion or individual writing for the abbreviations, individual writing for the remainder.
Notes: There are a number of writing tasks, but they are not intended to be done on the sheet itself.
Extension: Other writing activities can be based on the small ads not considered in the writing tasks on the sheet. Look at real small ads from a local paper, looking for other abbreviations. Funny mistakes in small ads will amuse the students and convey some useful points about sense, grammar and so on. Many books are available reproducing such 'howlers'.
Differentiation: Some students may be set just one of the writing tasks, such as the writing of the 'strange' small ad.
Linked pages: Persuasion 1 – Advertising p.74, Direct speech p.48, Letters 1 – Setting it out p.61.

Speech writing

Objective: Writing a one-minute speech.
Students: Class discussion followed by individual writing.
Notes: The suggested 120–140 words for a one-minute speech is for a smooth, rehearsed performance. Most students would not manage this number if reading from cold or extemporising. The exercise does depend on work being done on the performance of the speech.
Extension: The 'one minute' format could be applied to the work on 'Persuasion' and 'In my opinion'.
Differentiation: For some students the one minute rule may need to be relaxed and a rough word count employed instead. An interesting approach is for students to work in pairs, each preparing a speech for the other, and coaching each other on the performance.
Linked pages: Persuasion 1 – Advertising p.74, In my opinion p.20, Redrafting 2 – Prose p.35.

Interviewing

Objective: To prepare an interview, thinking about planned and supplementary questions.
Students: Groups of three.
Notes: This is mostly an oral activity, but interviewers will need to prepare three questions. Each member of the group should do this, then take it in turns to play the various rôles. This is a good activity for the teacher to assess speaking and listening skills.
Extension: This is an extemporised activity but it can be directed towards script writing.
Differentiation: Supplementary questions are

quite difficult and involve 'thinking on your feet'; practice and example by the teacher can help. The initial highlighting activity could be done by the class working with the teacher.
Linked pages: Questionnaire p.79, Playscript 1 p.56.

Questionnaire

Objective: The preparation of questions for a questionnaire about the school.
Students: Individual or group work.
Notes: Most surveys succeed or fail on the cogency of the questions rather than the answers. Introductory discussion is important to get students thinking about leading questions (Why do you think the food is so bad?) and questions where there is only one answer (Do you think the school could be improved?). Encourage questions that ask for ratings (On a scale of 0–10, how do you rate the sports facilities?).
Differentiation: The questions can be compiled as a group activity, perhaps working with a teacher/support teacher. The questions could then be written in and copies made for each member of the group. The questionnaire should be handed out for filling in, rather than used for an interview.
Linked pages: Interviewing p.78, Providing information 2 – Welcome to our school! p.72.

Autobiography 1 – A CV

Objective: Writing a CV.
Students: Individual work, though tick points could be worked through as a group.
Notes: The note making stage is the most important, and these notes shoudl be looked at carefully before the final CV is written. The final CV is an extension activity.
Linked pages: Note making 1 and 2 pp.9 and 10, Facts and opinions p.7, Working on notes p.8.

Autobiography 2 – I'm the sort of person that...

Objective: Providing a structure for a piece of 'confessional' writing.
Students: Individual writing after class discussion.
Notes: Encourage story telling (see 'Story telling – True stories') as the first stage of this activity.
Differentiation: This is a good activity for scribing by partners or for an initial telling on tape for later transcription.
Linked pages: Story telling – True stories p.12, Personal writing – *Me Jane* p.88.

Biography 1 – A friend

Objective: A piece of extended writing about a friend.
Students: Pair work, taking it in turns to ask questions and to take notes.
Notes: Ensure that the questions are written in draft before being written on the sheet. Long answers may need extra paper.
Differentiation: The number of questions can be reduced to three, for a shorter piece of writing. Try to encourage questions that provide information about the person's character rather than factual points about where they live, what food they like, and so on.
Linked pages: Questionnaire p.79, Autobiography 2 – I'm the sort of person that... p.81 (this makes a good linked activity producing material that can be included in the biography), Interviewing p.78.

Biography 2 – Someone famous

Objective: A small research project on a famous person, thinking about sources of information.
Students: Individual or pair work.
Notes: This sheet will lead into library or other research activities. Footballers, pop stars and other ephemeral personalities may not feature in the library, and students will have to think about how they are going to find their information.
Extension: Students could produce a 'celebrity feature' about their famous person in note form. Alternatively, an extended piece of writing could be produced either as a straight

account or as a first person narrative in which the writer imagines that he or she is the famous person.

Linked pages: Facts and opinions p.7, Listening and note making 1 and 2 pp.9 and 10, First person – Using 'I' p.108.

Direct speech

Match the words with the speech bubble. Put the matching number in the bubble.

1 You can't leave it there!
2 What on Earth are you doing here?
3 I can't stand the sight of you any more!
4 I'm not going anywhere!
5 Can't you find anything better to do?
6 Where did you say you come from?

Choose one of these conversations and write it using direct speech.

Indirect speech is used when a writer tells us what a speaker has said, but doesn't quote the exact words used. It is often used in newspaper reporting, because the reporter may not have written down the exact words and has to write a report from notes. Indirect speech does not use speech marks.

Gary to stay

Gary Collins (22) a footballer with Munchester City, denied today that he was intending to quit the game. He said that although the season had been poor and his form was currently dreadful, he was confident that matters would improve. His manager, Billy Rottweiller, defended his player and denied rumours of a free transfer to Sludgemouth Town, currently bottom of the league. Rottweiller said he had every confidence in Gary's ability and hoped that a break from the game would make all the difference.

Use one of these headlines to write a newspaper report. Use indirect speech.

School lunch incident – burger blamed

Lollipop lady foils gang

Shoplifting pop star shame

Headteacher blames results on the weather

Are they extra-terrestrials?

Story 1 - The missing section

This story has a missing section. Talk about what might happen in that section, then try and write it.

Abdul was thinking of nothing in particular as he waited in the post office queue. Four people waited in line in front of him. Friday was always busy, as many of the senior citizens collected their pensions on that day.

There was a crash from behind as the glass door of the post office burst open. Two men wearing stockings over their heads rushed in. One was carrying a bag. The other held a coat over his arm.

"Right! Flat on the floor and none of you will get get hurt!" yelled the man with the coat. "No funny business, I've got a gun!"

Abdul and the rest of the queue scrambled to the floor. The other man opened the bag.

"Give me the money!"

The terrified counter clerk started pushing notes underneath the glass window. The man with the coat stood directly over Abdul, threatening anyone who moved.

One of the old ladies started yelling. "You young thug! You won't get away with this!"
The man with the coat started yelling, and pointed the coat at the old woman. Abdul looked up. The coat had swung aside a little, and from where Abdul was on the floor he could see that the 'gun' was just a stick!

The old lady bravely continued shouting at the thieves. Angry now, the one with the fake gun strode over to hit her. But Abdul had firmly grabbed his leg and, unbalanced, the man fell over with a crash.

Abdul jumped up and tried to sit on the thief. "It's not really a gun" he yelled. The thief's partner abandoned his bag and set off to help. The rest of the queue, knowing that they would not be shot whatever happened, grabbed him and pulled him over.

The customers were a willing bunch but most of them were old. The thieves were tough and things might still have gone wrong if the police hadn't arrived at that moment, summoned by the alarm button the counter clerk had pushed.

The clerk and the customers in the post office were full of praise for Abdul as the two raiders were led away. "'Ee's a brave young lad" said the old woman who had shouted at the thieves. "'Ee deserves a medal for what 'e did."

Story 2 - Beginning, middle and end

Here are some sentences from the beginning, middle and end of two stories. They are muddled up. Sort out which sentence goes in which story, then put them in the right order.

A The door slammed shut behind them, hiding the dreadful secret.

B 'It's been a great evening. Shall we meet up on Saturday?'

C He had never seen her there before and she looked very lonely.

D The cellar was damp and cold and full of cobwebs.

E "I've just moved here with my family."

F The house hadn't been lived in for 40 years.

First story

Beginning

Middle

End

Second story

Beginning

Middle

End

Finish off these sentences.

The first story is about

The second story is about

Poetry 1 – What am I?

These four poems describe ordinary things in a surprising way. What are they describing?

I'm a
Rattler of pebbles,
A wrecker of ships,
A hiding place for octopuses,
A beach cleaner,
A blue mirror for the sky,
A greedy muncher of cliffs,
An angry beast foaming at the mouth...

What am I?

I'm a
Fruit maker,
A bird houser,
A swing supporter,
A leaf wearer,
A sad person waving goodbye in a storm...

What am I?

I'm a
Street washer,
An umbrella-opener,
A people annoyer,
A cricket match stopper,
A turner-up of coat collars...

What am I?

I'm a
Water jumper,
A short cut maker,
A traffic carrier,
I jump from one bank to another,
But sometimes my feet
Stay in the water!

What am I?

Try and finish off the poem below about the wind, then try a poem of your own. You could choose one of these ideas, or a new one of your own.

The sun　**Snow**　**A car**　**A TV set**　**An elephant**　**A school**

I'm a
Hat stealer,
A cloud pusher,

I'm a

Poetry 2 – Two-line poems

This poem is only two lines long!

A crisp bag swirling through the air;
An alien spaceship sucked into a black hole.

The **first line** describes what you actually see – a crisp bag.

The **second line** describes what it turns into in your imagination – an alien spaceship.

The first line ends with a semi-colon. This gives a long pause at the end of the line, to build up the suspense.

Here is another two-line poem by Michael. He had a rather gruesome idea.

The sea beating on the cliffs;
A thousand white rats gnawing open a coffin.

Here are some first lines for you to turn into something. Use your imagination!

An old newspaper flapping down the street;

____

Water gurgling down the plughole;

____

A football thudding into the back of the net;

____

Now try writing both lines yourself. You could work with a partner. Make up a first line each about something real, then swap your lines.

____

____

Poetry 3 – Syllables

Can you find the next animal in this list? Splitting the words up might help.

Cat	Cat
Rabbit	Rab bit
Antelope	An te lope
Caterpillar	Cat er pill ar

To find the answer, you need to count **syllables**. Add to these lists of animals, counting the syllables.

One syllable	Two syllables	Three syllables	Four syllables	Five syllables
cat	rabbit	antelope	caterpillar	
horse	monkey	kangaroo	alligator	

This poem is called a **haiku**. It has a special pattern of syllables.

A tree in autumn	(5 syllables)
Bends over like an old man	(7 syllables)
Who has lost his coins.	(5 syllables)

Try to finish these haiku.

The caterpillar
Pushes along the branch like

The disco lights flash

Poetry 4 – I am

Use this pattern for an **I am** poem of your own. You could write about old trains or planes, old clothes, old toys, old houses, or anything else old and worn out. You could make your poem have a happy ending by writing about something that will be given to someone who will care for it, or something that will be repaired and turned into something else.

I am an old Jaguar car.

Once I roared down the motorway,

Breaking the speed limits

And the hearts of motorists

Who couldn't afford a car like me.

My racing green paintwork

Was polished till it shone,

My chrome dazzled the slow

coaches

As I shot past.

But now I am a wreck.

My tyres are flat,

My bodywork is rusty,

My windscreen is broken.

Soon I will be cut up for scrap,

Melted down,

And used to make bean tins.

I am

Once

But now

Soon

Playscript 1

A **script** for a play or TV show is written in a very special way.

- Everything except the words actually spoken is in capital letters.
- The script must include instructions for the actors as well as their words.
- The script must include instructions for the producer of the play for such things as sound effects.

Read this playscript very carefully, then, using the same rules, continue with the scene. Come up with a cast list and a title for your script.

INTERIOR. SCHOOL CLASSROOM.

SCHOOL STUDENTS ARE WAITING FOR THE LESSON TO BEGIN. MOST ARE READING OR TALKING QUIETLY, ONE OR TWO ARE TRYING TO GET THEIR HOMEWORK FINISHED.

SIMON: (TURNING ROUND TO HELEN) I saw you going round to Steve's house last night.

HELEN: (LOOKING ANXIOUS) Shh! I don't want James to know about that.

SIMON: (GRINNING) So you're double timing James now, then.

HELEN: (ANGRILY) No, I'm not! I was just helping Steve with his homework.

SIMON: Oh yeah? Why is he busy doing his homework now then? (SHOUTS ACROSS TO STEVE) Hey Steve, were you too busy last night to do your homework then?

HELEN: (UPSET) I said shut up! (SHE THUMPS HIM ON THE BACK)

JAMES: (FROM THE BACK OF THE CLASS) What are you doing to Helen?

SIMON: I'm not doing anything! She hit me! I just asked why she was...

(HELEN THUMPS HIM AGAIN)

Playscript 2

Here are two pieces of writing. One is a newspaper story in **indirect speech**, the other is part of a story in **direct speech**.

Choose one to turn into a playscript. Remember that everything except the words actually spoken should be in capital letters.

Caught Red Handed

Police were called to a house in Oak Street yesterday where a man was seen climbing through a window. On arrival the police challenged the man and asked him what he was doing. He claimed to be the owner of the house who had lost his key. The police asked him why he was climbing out of the window with a video recorder if he was the owner of the house. The man said he was taking it to be mended. One of the neighbours told the police that he certainly wasn't the owner of the house, who was on holiday at the time. Although the man continued to claim he was innocent, he was arrested and taken to the police station.

Planet Explorers

The planet seemed Earth-like, and the atmosphere was breathable. The crew stepped out on to the planet.

"Great to breathe some real air for once," said Ted, breathing deeply. "I get fed up with canned air after the first month."

Captain Carson looked pleased. "This planet looks perfect for our new Earth colony. Good air, no dangerous natives…"

There was a twang and a clang as a spear bounced off the hull of the landing ship. Another spear missed Jade by a few centimetres and quivered in the ground.

"No dangerous natives, eh?" yelled Jade, as she led the rush back to the ship. "Perhaps those spears are their way of showing that they're pleased to see us!"

Ted looked puzzled. "I don't understand it. We spent days looking at this planet from space and there were no signs of intelligent life."

Jade glared at him. "They may not be intelligent, but they've got a pretty good aim. That thing nearly hit me!"

Meanwhile Captain Carson was looking out at the planet through the view port.
"Well would you believe that?" he said, astonished.

A hundred metres from the ship grew what looked like a red cactus with very long spines. As they watched, one of the spines shot into the air and hit the ship with a clang.

"Wow – intelligent plants!" gasped Ted.

Jade rushed out of the ship and returned with one of the 'spears'. "They're not weapons," she laughed. "They're seeds! The spears make sure they stick in the ground to give them a chance to grow!"

The captain groaned. "What about the new colony?" he said. "To live here you would need to wear armour all the time!"

Diary 1 – Long and short

Robert keeps two diaries. In the first one he makes quick notes every day. He writes a fuller account of what he has done at the weekend. Finish off the long diary entry for the day, using the information in the short diary.

Short diary

Tues Aug 3rd

A.M. Went shopping in Munchester. Couldn't find the jeans I was after. Rained all morning. Bus late - got soaked! Fish & Chips for lunch.

P.M. Went round to Simon. Still raining - couldn't go cycling. Played on computer instead.

Eve Boring! Aunt Jean came round. Went on and on about her operation. Couldn't hear the television...

Long diary

Tuesday August 3rd

When I got up it was pouring with rain, and I thought that I really couldn't be bothered to go into Munchester to buy my new jeans. Mum went on and on about my messy room after breakfast so I thought that I would go, just to get a bit of peace!

It was really chucking it down in Munchester and my left shoe started leaking. I went into every clothes shop in the place, but, typically, they either hadn't got the brand I wanted, or the size, or the colour. I was pretty fed up by the time I got back to the bus stop. I must have waited 20 minutes for the bus and I was soaked when I got on. At home everyone was too busy tidying up the place for Aunt Jean's visit to get any lunch on so I went down to the chippy and bought fish and chips all round.

Diary 2 – Making it interesting

Diaries can be very boring! Here is an example of a boring diary.

Wednesday 3rd October.

Got up. Raining. Went to school. Morning; Double maths, science, geography. Burger and chips for lunch. Got into an argument with Barry. Afternoon, drama, P.E. Forgot my kit so I got a detention. Watched TV all evening till bed time.

Even on an ordinary day, enough funny or surprising things happen to make an interesting diary. You can always add your thoughts about the things that are going on, and your impressions of the people you meet, like this:

Another wet day! I'm really fed up with the weather at the moment. There's a big puddle just outside the school and Mr Jenkins got splashed by a car as he walked past. That made my day!

Barry is such an idiot. He went on and on about how great his new bike is, waving his hands about all over the place ...

Try this now with your diary of yesterday. Fill in this time chart to help you remember what happened before you start your really interesting diary entry.

7 a.m. ....

....

8 a.m. ....

....

9 a.m. ....

....

10 a.m. ....

....

11 a.m. ....

....

12 noon ....

....

1 p.m. ....

....

2 p.m. ....

....

3 p.m. ....

Continue over the page.

....

Letters and envelopes

Mr and Mrs J Smith
'Sea View'
Factory Rd
Easton
STRATFORD-ON-AVON
Warwickshire
CV46 9BH

Notice:

- The address is not too far up the envelope – otherwise the postmark will be printed over it.
- The nearest main town (called the post town) is in capital letters.
- The post code has been included. This helps to speed up the mail.

38 Conifer Gardens
Weston
BASINGSTOKE
Hampshire
RG33 9DP

The Head Teacher
Southdown Secondary School
Paradise St
Upperville
MILTON KEYNES
Bucks
MK22 4DY

22nd May 1995

Dear Madam,

Notice:

- The address the letter is *from* is top right, the address it is *going to* is lower down on the left. You don't need to include the receiver's address if you are writing to a friend.
- The letter has a date.
- The addresses are written correctly, including the postcode.
- The letter starts correctly. If you don't know the name of the person you are writing to, put 'Dear Madam' or 'Dear Sir'. If you are not sure whether they are male or female you could put 'Dear Sir or Madam,' or something like 'Dear Head Teacher'.

Practise envelope writing and starting letters. Compare your letters and envelopes with these.

Letters 1 - Setting it out

Writing a correctly set out letter is very important. How we set it out depends on what sort of letter it is. Look at the types of letter in list A. For each one, decide which items in list B would be suitable. Write the numbers next to the sorts of letter. One of them is done for you. If none are quite right, write in your own idea.

List A

Note for the milkman

Job application **1 5 7 12**

Postcard from holiday to a parent

Letter to a sick relative in hospital

Letter to a company complaining about shoddy goods

Letter to a teacher apologising for your behaviour

Letter to a TV star asking for an autograph

Letter to a newspaper

Letter to an elderly uncle who might leave you a fortune in his will

A letter asking someone to marry you

List B

1 Stamped addressed envelope
2 Your full address at the top right
3 A shortened address to the right
4 No address
5 The address of the person you are writing to on the left
6 Start Dear Sir
7 Start Dear Sir or Madam
8 Start Dear (first name only)
9 Start Dear Mr/Mrs .....
10 Start My Darling .....
11 Don't start with anything
12 Finish with Yours faithfully
13 Finish with Yours sincerely
14 Finish with Love from
15 Finish with Best wishes
16 Just write or sign your name

Which letter from List A is this? Can you finish it off?

34 West Street
Whiteston
MUNCHESTER
Dorset
DT3 5LH

Klondike Computers Ltd
Southbridge Industrial Estate
WINNERTON
Hampshire
SO22 5LY

22nd May 1995

Dear Sir,

Letters 2 - Getting that job

Talk about this job application letter, then work on a version that you think is more likely to get Kev the job.

To: Mick
Flat 7,
Dorian House,
Cemona Estate,
Boltham.

Wed. 3rd December 1987

Dear Mick,

As I was checking out the local rag just now, I spotted your ad for a lead singer for your band, and I thought wow! that's just the kinda thing I've been looking for. I've always been really into music, specially rock & progressive stuff, and for a long time now I've been thinking of forming a band of my own called The Apricots. The drag is, none of the guys I hang out with are muzo's. My mate Rick plays piano, but he only knows dudes like Shopan and Chykovski, which is just too square man. The kind of bands I'm into at the moment are Level 42 and Dire Straits, but being into all kinds of music, I can get into anything really, so it doesn't matter if your band doesn't sound like Level 42.

As for the singing experience, I guess you could say I've had plenty, as I've been singing all my life. I really dig it. I always sing in the bath and when I'm on the loo, and when my parents are out, I practice poses with the kitchen brush in front of the mirror. I've worked out some pretty cool moves that I think would look good on stage. All my mates say I've got a good voice and that I should join a band, so when I saw the ad I thought, go for it!

I guess I'm quite good looking (or so my girlfriend says) and although I'm not very tall, I would probably wear high-heeled boots on stage which would effectively get over this point. Also, I wouldn't mind wearing make-up, as I know that under bright stage lights, your face looks dead pale.

So man, I'd be glad to come in for an audition next time you're rehearsing, as long as you let me know what songs you're doing in advance, then I can learn them off the records.

Look forward to hearing from you.

Chow,

Kev Daughtry.

P.S. Sorry, I don't have my own transport, but with a bus pass I can get just about anywhere in Greater Manchester.

'In Reply to Your Advertisement' by John Kirkbride, Scholastic Publications Ltd 1989

Your local garden centre is advertising for Saturday staff. What skills do you think they require? Write a letter to apply for the job.

Letters 3 - Complaining

Trevor Bryant saw this in a holiday brochure. It sounded good, so he booked his holiday.

> ## Hotel Luxxo
>
> Relax by day at the side of our two almost Olympic size swimming pools! Dance away the night in our ballroom, with regular discos. We have two bars serving drinks at very reasonable prices. Eat our superb meals prepared by international chefs. At Hotel Luxxo, our guests come first and nothing is too much trouble to make your stay a happy one!

Here is an extract from Trevor's diary.

> Thursday, July 19th
>
> This hotel is a real dump! I shall write and complain when I get home. One of the pools is empty being repainted, it's a paddling pool for toddlers and the other is small and so crowded you can't get near it. There hasn't been a disco yet. The prices are horrendous - I buy coke from the town and bring it back to my room. One of the managers saw me bring it in and he started swearing at me - I think he was drunk.
>
> When I got up this morning I trod on a cockroach with my bare foot. I didn't bother to go for breakfast. The food is so disgusting even the cockroaches have given up and they've all come to my room instead...

Trevor booked his hotel through Speedy Tours Ltd, 57 High Steet, MUNCHESTER, Dorset DT33 4RY. Write a polite, correctly set out letter of complaint, demanding the return of some of the money.

Speech bubbles

These are the words for the speech bubbles. They are muddled up, and two of them don't come from this story at all! Sort them out and put the letter in the correct bubble.

A That was fun!
B I knew this would happen.
C You're going too fast!
D I'm quite safe.
E He's up there!
F Don't you know it's dangerous to allow children to climb trees?
G Get down from there!
H Look out!
I Help! I'm stuck!
J Don't worry, he'll be down in a minute.
K I can't hold on much longer!

Reportage 1 – Reporter's notebook

An important government minister was visiting Munchester to open a new section of road. Many people were angry about the road and had come along to protest. The chief news reporter on the Munchester Echo was at the scene with her notebook. Here are her notes and her final news report.

Tues 3rd April
Minister Mr Henry Traffycone MP, arr. 10.30 a.m.
Started speech bfore cuttng tape.
Protesters in Crowd started chanting
Countryside Murderer
Down with roads
Down with cars
Minister continued with speech…
wonderful new opportunity for
Munchster – end of traffic congestion
in tn cntre...marvelous
achievment...Protester threw egg –
hit mnister on face. More eggs fly.
Bag of flour. Minster hustled away.
Arrests made.
Mnster returns later & cuts tape.

It's pancake time for Minister

The minister for roads, The Right Honorable Henry Traffycone, MP, was struck with eggs and flour at the opening ceremony for the Munchester by-pass yesterday.
Mr Traffycone (78) spoke of the benefits for Munchester of a traffic free town centre and the marvellous job done by the contractors who finished the job less than two years late. The speech was difficult to hear against a constant chanting of 'down with roads' and other slogans from the protesters.
The Minister was unable to finish his speech as the missiles were now raining down. An egg hit him on the side of his head, and flour covered his suit.
Once all the protesters had been dragged away to the police cells Mr Traffycone bravely returned to cut the tape and declare the road open.

Work with a partner. Look at the list of news reports below. Choose one each. Imagine you are at the scene and write notes on what you saw. Pass your notes to your partner to write out as a headline story.

Plane crash **Riot at football match**

Freak storm damages coastal town

Girl beats world record

Reportage 2 – Sports report

Johnson misses by inches

Munchester 1 Westford 1

by Mike Smart

Bob Johnson missed scoring by inches on Saturday.

The tough Welshman has waited six months to return to City after a serious back injury.

He admitted that his miss may cost him his team place when Lenny Cartwright returns from suspension next week.

Johnson, who hit the Westford woodwork in the 44th minute, said that someone would take his place if he kept hitting the post.

It was a bad day for City with winger Charlie Croft hitting the same spot three minutes from time with a powerful 20 yard effort. City's 100 per cent home record has now gone despite a hatful of chances.

SLICK

In the first half Rupe Marston threatened to storm Westford with his slippery skills.

The slick striker was on the spot in the 23rd minute to head home a cross from Archer after Stewart had won a crucial mid-field tussle.

The Westford defence struggled in the air but amazingly Westford's Jake Scott proved aerial master at the other end in the 38th minute. He rose to thump a header from a Steve White corner into the back of the net.

OFFSIDE

Westford should have taken the lead in the 42nd minute when left back Brian Marchant had a perfectly good goal disallowed for offside.

City boss Luke Stagg admitted that his team had made mistakes.

"I genuinely thought we could win this game. We exposed them but couldn't apply the finishing touches."

Read this newspaper account of a football match.

Notice:

- A headline about the most interesting thing that happened, followed by the result.
- The 'by-line' (the name of the person who wrote the story).
- First sentence in bold type. This repeats the most interesting thing.
- Very short paragraphs.
- 'Mini' headlines to make it easier to read.
- A quote from the manager to round the report off.

Use this plan to write your own sports report. Here are some ideas:

- A real sporting event that you watched, live or on television.
- A school event.
- An imaginary event. You could even make up the sport. What about inter-galactic meteor bowling?

Describing places 1 – Planning it out

This is a talk by Samantha following a visit to an activity centre.

> Weston Park Activity Centre is a great place to go if you like outdoor activities. It is a large area by the river with fields, a wood, lots of different buildings and the river running through. There are lots of water activities on the river or in the swimming pool. Canoeing and rowing take place on the river, but not swimming. It's a bit cold for that! The centre has its own stable and horses for riding, places for archery, and a track through the wood and along the river for orienteering and mountain biking. When you're not doing all that there's an assault course you can try. When you first go there, you can have a go at lots of things until you find the thing you like best. The only drawback to Weston Park is that it costs quite a lot to go there. You just have to keep nagging at your parents until they come up with the cash!

Samantha was asked to prepare her talk carefully first. Notice that:

- The first two sentences gave her listeners 'the whole picture' before she started on the details.
- She tried to make her talk interesting by not being too serious.
- She came up with a good ending.

Samantha's class asked her questions about the place she had described.

Think of two questions you would have asked.

____

____

____

____

____

Think of a place you could describe to your class. Make notes on your place, then write out your first sentences that give the 'whole picture' of the place before you start on the detail.

____

____

____

____

____

Continue on the back of this sheet.

Describing places 2 – Good and bad

Here are two descriptions of Munchester.

1. Munchester is a wonderful town to live in. There are many beautiful old buildings and churches, and plenty of parks with well looked after flower beds. The choice of shops is good, and there is plenty of parking. There are many activities available, such as flower arranging, bowls...
2. Munchester is an awful place. There's no cinema, and the only places you can meet are out on the streets or in pubs. The shops are all boring. The buses stop running at half past eight at night, so you can't get into town in the evening without getting a lift. There's just nothing to do at all...

Talk about these two descriptions. Why do you think they are so different? What sort of person wrote each one?

All places have good and bad features. Sometimes this depends on your point of view.

Choose a place such as your village, town or city, your school, or another place you know well. List good points and bad points.

Good points	**Bad points**

Write two short accounts of your place. One should encourage people to go there, the other piece should put people off.

Instructions 1 – Cassette recorder

Here are the operating buttons of a cassette recorder.

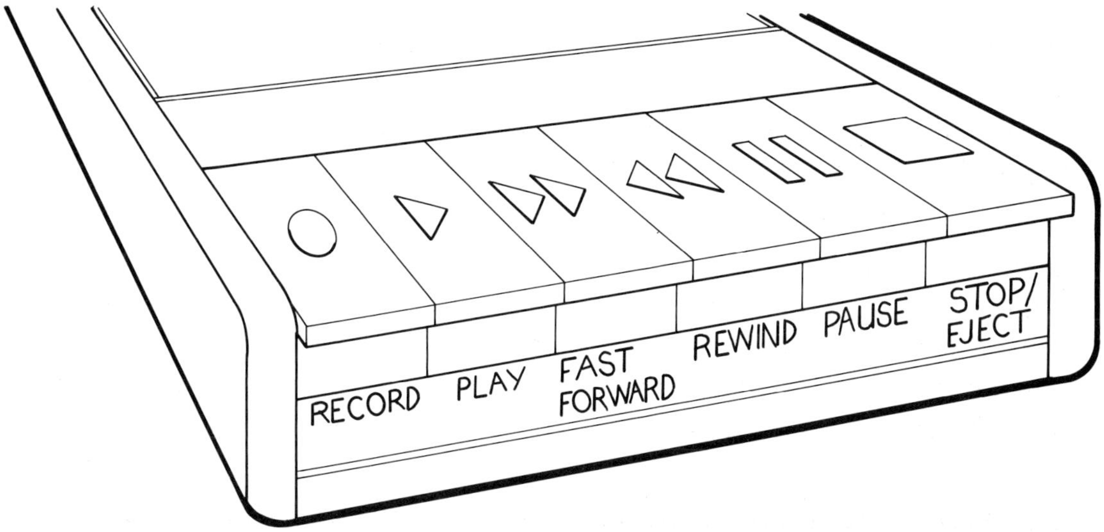

Write the operating instructions in note form. Make your instructions as simple and as clear as possible.

How to operate your new Blastertone cassette recorder

Instructions 2 – Feeding the pet

Dawn is going on holiday. Her friend Justin has agreed to feed and look after her pet while she is away. He doesn't know that Dawn's pet is a little unusual!

Choose an unusual pet from the pictures below, then finish off Dawn's letter.

36 Tadpole Street
Burnham
WESTPOOL
Hants
SO34 9PH

3rd August

Dear Justin,
Thank you very much for agreeing to look after Dennis for me. There are some things you need to know.

Providing information 1 – Fire!

This poster explains what to do if there is a fire at Redlawn School. Unfortunately, Redlawn is a junior school and the notice is too difficult for the children to read. Design a more effective poster using this information.

Action in the event of fire

1 On discovering a fire, the nearest alarm should be sounded and a responsible adult informed.

2 If it is possible and does not carry undue risk, the fire should be tackled by a responsible adult <u>only</u> using the apparatus provided.

3 The fire brigade should be summoned by dialing 999.

4 On hearing the alarm, the building should be vacated by the nearest exit.

5 Classes should assemble on the large playground, where those responsible for each class should call a register and ascertain the whereabouts of any missing person.

6 No person should re-enter the building for any purpose unless the fire brigade has assured them that it is safe to do so.

Useful facts about the school

Address ________________________________

____

Telephone number ________________________________

Head Teacher ________________________________

Number of pupils attending the school ________________________________

Daily times ________________________________

Clothing to be worn to school ________________________________

____

Meal information ________________________________

____

How to get to the school ________________________________

____

Welcome to our school!

Providing information 3 – Packaging

This is the packaging for a wonderful new product. It may be a sweet bar, a new electrical gadget, a new food, a new washing powder or something for DIY.

Choose one of these products, or one of your own.

When you design your wrapper, which of these things will you need? Tick the boxes.

- a product name ☐
- size or weight ☐
- a picture of what is inside ☐
- an advertising slogan ☐
- instructions ☐
- bar code ☐
- a safety warning ☐
- list of ingredients ☐
- nutritional information ☐
- special offer panel ☐
- manufacturer's name and address ☐

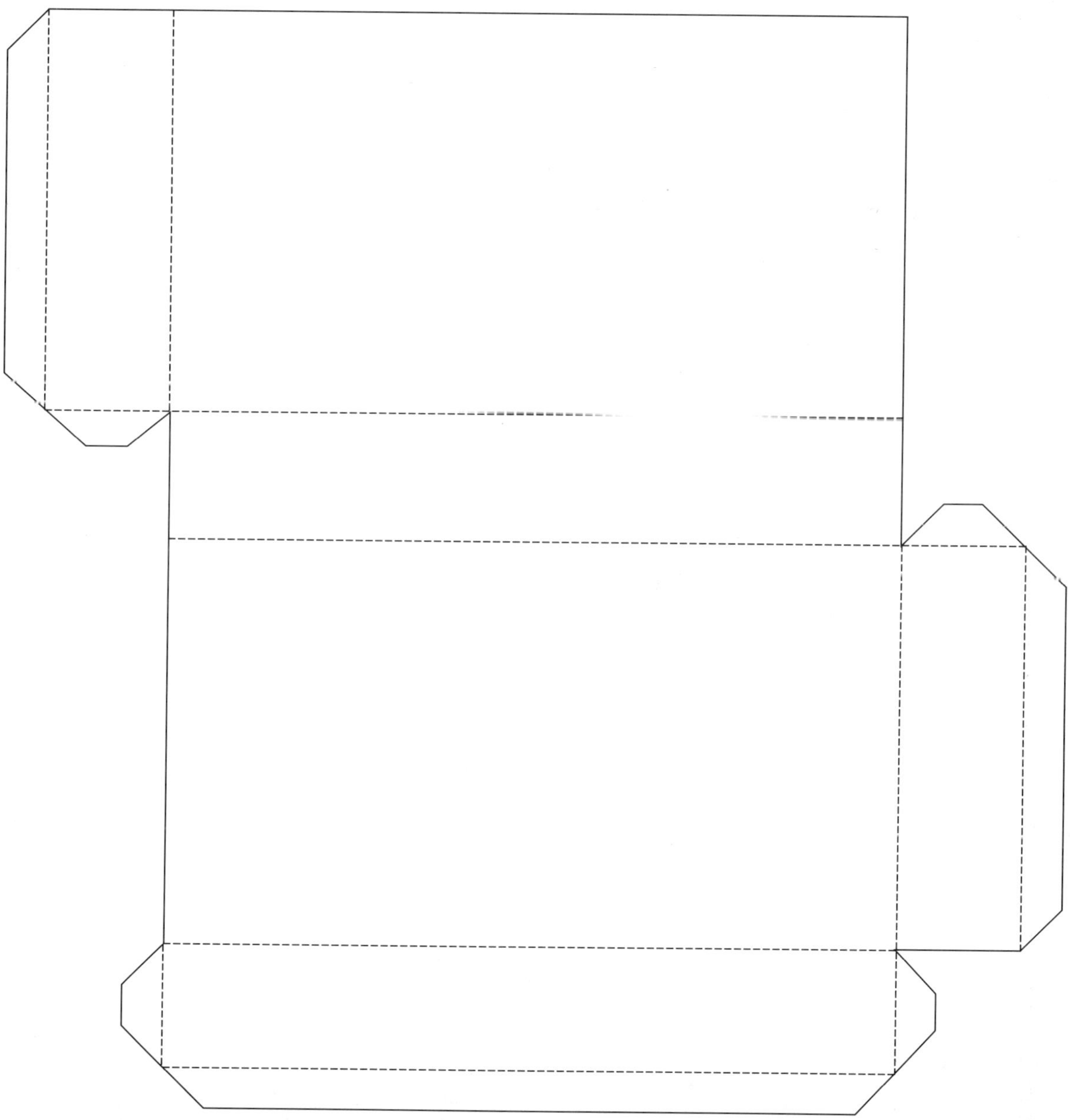

Persuasion 1 – Advertising

Advertisements have to obey strict rules. This is to make sure people aren't misled.

An advertisement must:

- be truthful
- not offend anyone
- not rubbish other products.

Drink new

Full-O-Fruit

The natural fruity drink! Full of orchard goodness!

It's delicious – and good for you!

Guaranteed to make you live longer! Protects teeth and gums!

The ultimate drink sensation – better than Croakola, tastes as good as Champagne!

Brilliant orange and purple can – you can really annoy stupid, middle-aged people by chucking it down in the street!

Here is the ingredients list from a can of Full-O-Fruit.

Water, Carbon Dioxide, Artificial flavourings, Artificial colour (E102, E104), Preservative.

This advertisement was banned. Talk about why this might have happened. Plan a better advertisement for this new fizzy drink in the box below. Do you need to change its name?

Persuasion 2 – Junk food

Samantha has strong views on the subject of junk food on sale at school.

> School meals should be much healthier than they are at the moment. Every day there are piles of chips, sausages, burgers and cream buns for sale, but hardly any salads and healthy foods such as fresh fruit and vegetables. Baked potatoes and brown rice would be much better for everybody than chips. Foods that are high in fat can lead to heart disease and other health problems, and people who don't eat any fresh food can miss out on important vitamins.
>
> People say that they should be allowed to choose what they like, and not have healthy food forced on them if they don't like it and don't want it. They say that chips and cream buns can't do you any harm.
>
> I think they are wrong. People often eat what they are used to, and won't try new things which they might actually like better. If there were no chips on sale people would have to try other things, and they might find that they really like them. In years to come these people would be really grateful that they had been made to eat healthy food, especially when they see people who have eaten chips all their lives overweight, or in hospital, or dead!

Samantha's piece of writing is in three parts.

1. She outlined her point of view in the first sentence, then explained it.
2. She thought about what people who diasgreed with her would say.
3. She said why she disagrees with them and put forward a strong final point. (This is sometimes called 'the clincher').

Plan a piece of writing of your own putting forward a point of view. There are some starter ideas at the bottom of the page. Follow the 'three point' plan, and try to include a good 'clincher'.

Ideas for your writing:

School Uniforms

Cruelty to animals

Drug taking

Watching too much TV

Unfair parents

Persuasion 3 – Small ads

Here is part of the small advertisements section of a local newspaper.

Small ads

For sale. Wedding dress size 16. Never worn. 01564 345915

Free to good home. Large and lively Rottweiller dog. Muggins, 25 West Street, Munchester.

For sale. Colour TV set, v.g. cond, 22inch. £25 ono. 01957 483279 (ask for Tony)

Corns or other foot problems? Qualified chiropodist available. Rsnble rates. Ring Karen on 01234 543644

Roofing, guttering specialists. No job too small. 01985 785379

Computer games for Atari system. Fang of Doom, Mutant Gerbils, many others. £5 ea. Ring Bob on 01977 57894

Ford Fiesta Popular 1986. Txd, long MOT, good runner £450 ovno. 01879 5632

Wanted. Any records or tapes by Barry Manilow. Gd prices offered by collector. 01786 42568

Wanted urgently. Wedding dress. Must be size 16 and in gd condition. Ring June on 01453 879435

These advertisements have a number of abbreviations. Explain what they mean.

V.g. cond ______________________ Gd ______________________

ono ______________________ Txd ______________________

MOT ______________________ ovno ______________________

Rsnble ______________________ ea ______________________

Small ads are very short because they are paid for by the word or letter.

Here is an advertisement drafted by someone who has something to sell.

```
I have a really excellent drum kit for
sale. It has many extras and is absolutely
brilliant. It cost me over £500 but it is
for sale for only £300, or very near
offer. If you are interested ring Jim on
01987 657436.
```

Help Jim to save money by shortening his advertisement.

- The owner of the dog in the small ad does not have a phone. Write a letter asking for more details of the animal.
- You have something strange to sell or an odd service to offer. Write out your small ad. Use no more than ten words.
- You go and look at the Ford Fiesta and find that it is a bit of a wreck. You try and make the owner take a much lower price. Use direct speech to write your conversation with the owner.

Speech writing

You are going to prepare a talk that lasts just one minute.

A one-minute speech has between 120 and 140 words in it.

Ben planned out a talk on a TV programme that he had seen the night before. This was his plan.

1 Name of programme.

2 Type of programme.

3 People who were in it.

4 Outline of what happened in the show.

5 Opinion of the programme, and why.

This is Ben's one-minute talk:

Last night I watched *Grab it and Run*. This is a new game show on BCC 1. The host is Izzy Grabbet. The idea is that two people act out well-known phrases without speaking, and the other person guesses what the phrase is. For example, one group was given 'Give us a kiss for Christmas' and they mimed each word until the third person in their team guessed. It was difficult to mime 'Christmas!' The best team went through to the final where they had to guess a phrase performed by a celebrity. Last night Duane Dunkett was the celebrity. They got it right, and won a holiday to Tunisia.

I thought the programme was quite funny, but not very original, because I have seen shows just like it before.

Use Ben's plan for a one-minute speech of your own about a TV programme. If you choose a film or TV drama, don't try and tell the whole story – this will be very difficult in one minute. Try and sum up the story in just two or three sentences.

Try one-minute talks on other subjects. Always remember to plan your talk before you write it, and count the number of words you have used.

Interviewing

An interviewer does not just read out a set of questions, although he or she will always have a list to help them. A good interviewer will make up instant questions based on what the person they interview says. They can't plan these out in advance, because they don't know what will be said. Questions made up on the spot are sometimes called supplementary questions.

Here is part of the script of an interview. Highlight or underline the **planned** questions in one colour, and the **supplementary** questions in another.

Interviewer	Why did you decide to appear in this film? It is not your usual sort of rôle.
Big Star	I felt that I needed a change. I did make a comedy film some years ago, and enjoyed it very much.
Interviewer	What film was that?
Big Star	The Truth about Bananas. I co-starred with June Day.
Interviewer	Why is the film being made in Britain instead of America?
Big Star	The studios here were available at a good price, and the climate is perfect for the location shooting.
Interviewer	The British weather is perfect?
Big Star	That's right – in this film it rains all the time.
Inteviewer	That can't be very pleasant for the actors!
Big Star	That's right – we've all got colds already.

Work in groups of three. One person should play the interviewer, another the person interviewed, and the third person should be the TV viewer. The interviewer should prepare three questions to ask the person to be interviewed. Base them on what you know of the person. During the interview the TV viewer should time how long it lasts, then fill in the answers to these questions.

1 How many supplementary questions were asked after question 1?

2 How many after question 2?

3 How many after question 3?

4 How long did the interview last?

Give the interviewer and the person interviewed a grade based on this scale:

A Very well done

B Quite well done

C Average

D Not very good

E Room for improvement!

Questionnaire

You have decided to conduct a survey about how your school could be improved. You will need to think of six questions, leaving room on the sheet for answers.
Hints: Questions that can be answered yes or no are not very helpful.
You could say 'If your answer is no, please explain why'.
You are looking for suggestions, not just complaints.

Use this sheet to design your questionnaire. Try it out on a friend.

School improvement questionnaire

Prepared by ______________________________

Filled in by ______________________________

Please answer all the questions.

1 ______________________________

2 ______________________________

3 ______________________________

4 ______________________________

5 ______________________________

6 ______________________________

Thank you for your time.

Autobiography 1 – A CV

Sometimes you have to write a serious account of yourself so that other people can find out about you. This account is called a CV.
Write down three occasions when you might have to write a CV.

1 ______________________________

2 ______________________________

3 ______________________________

Here are ten pieces of advice to describe what a CV should be like. Tick the good ideas, and put a cross next to any bad advice.

Should be honest. ☐

Should include information on exam results and other achievements. ☐

Should list your main interests. ☐

Should describe your family and parents. ☐

Should exaggerate your good qualities and not mention any weaknesses. ☐

Should be neatly written, with no mistakes. ☐

Should be written by your Mum. ☐

Should give your views on such things as politics and the state of the world today. ☐

Should describe your ambitions. ☐

Should be funny, if possible. ☐

Before you write the final draft of your CV you should:

- Make notes of what should go in. (You may need to look up things like dates.)
- Write a first draft.
- Check it through carefully – get help if necessary.

Use this box for your notes. Use your answers to the questions to help you.

Continue over the page.

Autobiography 2 – I'm the sort of person that...

Here is an account by Sarah of something that happened to her.

> I'm the sort of person that is always doing stupid things, especially when other people are looking. I'm not really clumsy, it's just that things always happen to me. Once I had a banana yoghurt for lunch and I couldn't get the top off. I tugged and tugged at the lid and it came off all of a sudden. I had banana yoghurt all over me! Everyone was laughing. I was really embarrassed!

Here is Justin's story:

> I'm the sort of person that doesn't like getting up in the morning, though I don't mind sitting up late at night. In the holidays my mum gives me a shout to wake me up before she goes to work. Sometimes I go to sleep again! Once I heard my mum shouting from downstairs and I called out "See you tonight Mum". She came storming up the stairs because I'd slept all day and she had just got home!

Use this pattern for a piece of writing of your own. It helps to tell the story to someone before you start writing. Write a first draft in the box.

I'm the sort of person that

Once I

Biography 1 – A friend

If you are writing about a friend, you will need to include:

- facts you already know about them
- facts you need to find out about them
- what they think of themselves
- what you think of them.

Think of six questions to ask your friend to help you with your piece of writing. Ask about those things you don't already know.

Question 1 ______________________________

Answer ______________________________

Question 2 ______________________________

Answer ______________________________

Question 3 ______________________________

Answer ______________________________

Question 4 ______________________________

Answer ______________________________

Question 5 ______________________________

Answer ______________________________

Question 6 ______________________________

Answer ______________________________

Use the answers, the facts you already know, and your opinions for a short piece of writing about your friend. The ideas in the box may help you.

appearance	interests	character	
things they do that show what sort of person they are			
their life-story	ambitions	opinions	weaknesses
annoying habits	the way they talk	what makes them angry	

Biography 2 – Someone famous

Writing about a famous person is not as easy as writing about a friend. It is not always possible to interview them. They might be:

- difficult to get hold of or not willing to give interviews
- a long way away
- dead!

You will need to research information about your famous person. List possible places where you might find useful facts about these types of famous people.

A footballer ______________________

A pop singer ______________________

A politician ______________________

A king or queen from the past ______________________

Fill in this box with your research notes.

Famous person I want to research ______________________

Possible sources of information ______________________

What I would like to find out ______________________

Section 4 Section

Writing styles

The sheets in this section look at various styles of writing appropriate for different contexts. Work on dialect is included although, strictly speaking, this is not an aspect of style.
Style is a difficult concept for students who find language work difficult and who may still be struggling with the nuts and bolts, but the concept of formal and informal should not be too difficult to follow. The teacher will need other examples of formal/informal/dialect writing to back up what is offered here.

Using the worksheets

Formal and informal 1

Traffic accident

Objective: To write about the same imaginary incident in a formal and informal way.
Students: Individual work. Alternatively, students could work in pairs, with one writing the formal account and the other the informal account of an accident. The accounts can then be exchanged and rewritten in the alternative style.
Extension: The same plan can be used for writing about a real incident in the school, the formal one intended as an account for a school magazine.
Differentiation: The informal stage could be produced on tape, perhaps using interviewing techniques.
Linked pages: Interviewing p.78, Letters and envelopes (for the formal account) p.60, Redrafting 2 – Prose p.35.

Formal and informal 2

Invitations

Objective: To write invitations to a formal and an informal occasion.
Students: Individual work.
Notes: There are a number of formal words and phrases (such as 'request the pleasure of your company') that need to be introduced and understood.
Linked pages: Thesaurus p.30, Formal and informal 1 – Traffic accident p.86, Desk top publishing p.132.

Personal writing

Me Jane

Objective: To look at a casual style of personal writing.
Students: Classwork to read and discuss the extract, individual writing.
Notes: The style is 'formally incorrect' in that it is often written in non sentences. Discuss this with students. Try and bring out the idea of 'writing to show how you think' or how you would chat to a friend. Stress that this is not 'writing as you think' and that it is in fact very carefully thought out. Talk about how the reader is brought in almost as a friend of the character telling the story.
Differentiation: Writing like this is not as easy at it looks! Transcribing a taped story telling session is a good way in.
Linked pages: Story telling – True stories p.12, Autobiography 2 – I'm the sort of person that… p.81, First Person – Using 'I' p.108.

Using dialect

Joby

Objective: Looking at language variation through dialect.
Students: Group work.
Notes: There is a clear distinction that should be made between dialect and accent. Accent or speech variation is sometimes shown by non standard orthography (gunna = going to). Dialect involves non-standard grammar and vocabulary. The emphasis in this exercise is on vocabulary rather than grammar.
Extension: Use tape and video to show a wider range of dialect.
Linked pages: American English p.90, Slang p.91.

American English

Objective: Looking at differences between British and American English.

Students: Individual or group work, followed by individual writing.
Differentiation: The passage is quite a difficult one and should be read out before students are asked to read it silently. Try and bring out the Americanisms in your reading – practise first! The highlighting can be done as a group activity. The writing task can include dialect or non-standard spelling, but if you feel this is confusing it is best avoided.
Linked pages: Using dialect – *Joby* p.89, Thesaurus p.30.

SLANG

Objective: Looking at contemporary slang.
Students: Group work, followed by individual writing.
Notes: This extract will probably seem very dated in a very short time! It can be replaced by a piece from a current teenage pop magazine. Talk about contemporary words of approbation – examples in the passage are 'happenin', 'wicked' and 'unsad'. A translation of the extract for readers over the age of 16 is provided on the sheet.
Differentiation: The passage needs to be read aloud, but the teacher may feel uncomfortable in doing this! Ask a student to prepare a reading, giving help with any difficult words.
Linked pages: Thesaurus p.30, Direct speech p.48.

Formal and informal 1 – Traffic accident

On the way to school you saw a road traffic accident. No one was hurt, but two cars were badly damaged. One of the drivers asked for your name and address as a witness.

The first box below shows how you started to tell your friends about the accident.

The second box shows how you started to write a statement for the driver's insurance company.

The words in the word box will help you finish off these pieces of writing. Which words will be most suitable for each piece of writing? (Some will be useful in both.)

bashed
collided
fantastic
braked
speeding
loony
serious
fault
careless
a right madman
slippery
belting along

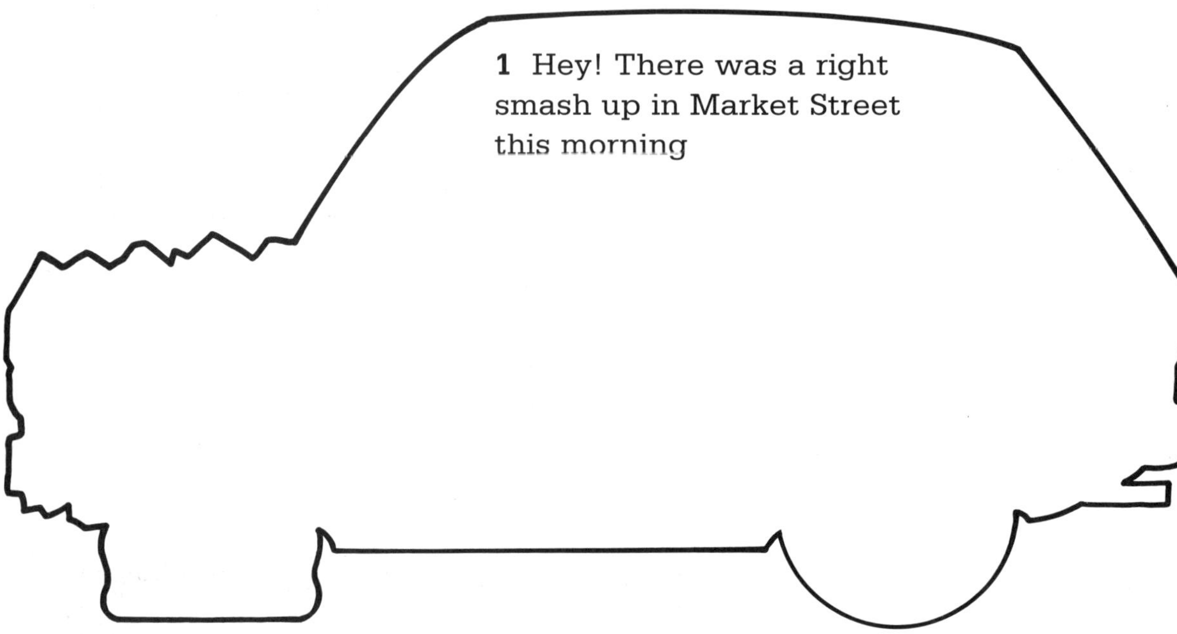

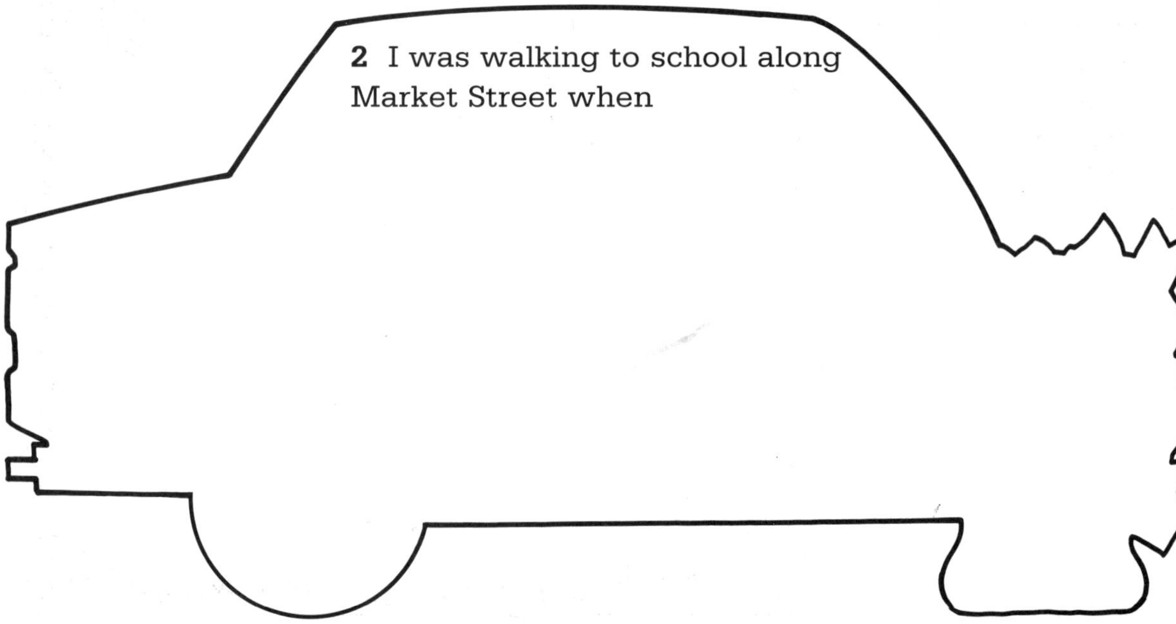

Formal and informal 2 – Invitations

One of these boxes has words from a wedding invitation. The other has words from a party invitation.

Which is which?

Design the full invitations in these boxes.

Jill and Mike

bring a bottle

fancy dress

7.30

Mr and Mrs

pleasure

company

request

son

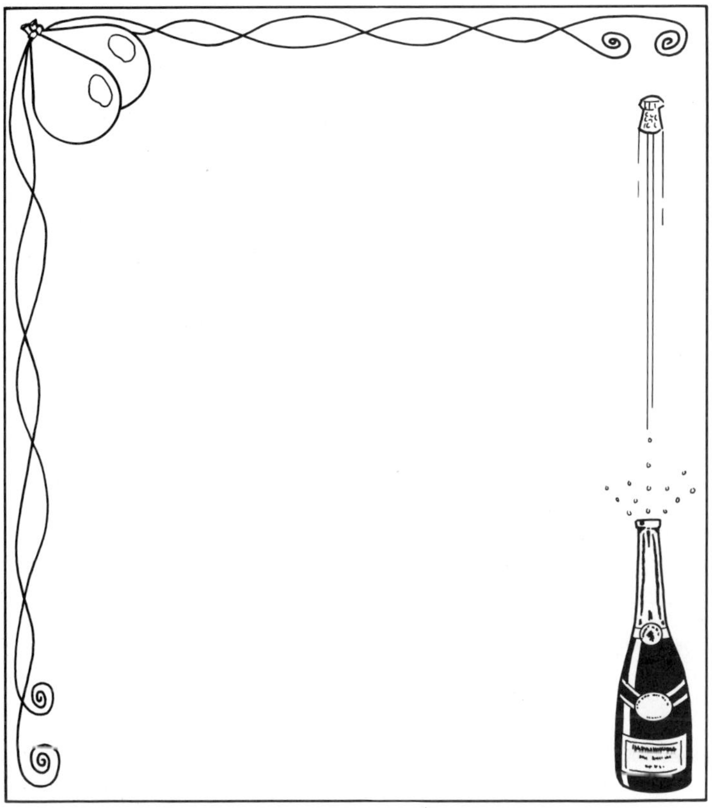

Here are some more invitations you could try:

- a party to celebrate a 100th birthday
- a school concert or play
- the opening of a new supermarket.

Personal writing - *Me Jane*

Read this extract. It comes from *Me Jane* by Sue Limb.

Many Happy Returns

Here it was. My birthday. Fifteen. My mum had promised me that by the time I was fifteen, my hips would've slimmed right down. But they hadn't. I bumped the right one on the bathroom doorpost as usual. It's black and blue. The hip, not the doorpost. I think one day I won't be able to get through the door at all. My mum says don't be daft, it'll all melt away. But nothing melts away with me. Except Larry Payne.

Larry Payne's really – but I mustn't start drooling about him. He's two classes above me at school, and I'm – but I mustn't. Anyway now I'm fifteen I'm going to ignore him. I've had enough pain and anguish. The thing is, he doesn't even know I exist. Just as well, says Ginger Mike, or it'd give him nightmares.

Points to notice:

- The girl (Jane) seems to be chatting to the reader in a casual way. How does Sue Limb make it sound like someone talking?
- It is a very truthful piece of writing. Jane makes two confessions. One is that she is overweight – what is the other?

Work on a piece of 'personal writing' of your own.

You may not want to write a piece of work like this because you don't want to give away your secrets! Remember, Sue Limb is not writing about herself. She made up a character called Jane. You could make up your own character. Perhaps you could use some of your own experiences in the writing.

Using dialect – *Joby*

Read this extract from *Joby* by Stan Barstow.
Joby is at the cinema. His friend Gus is firing pellets from a rubber band. One of the pellets hits the attendant.

"You there. Was it you?"
Joby blinked in the light of the torch, the grin gone from his face.
"Who, me?"
"Yes, you. Come on out here."
"I haven't done owt," Joby said.
"We'll see about that." The attendant took Joby by the arm.
"But I'm gunna miss the serial," Joby protested.
"You should ha' thought about that before."
Joby was marched downstairs into the foyer. The woman in the pay-box was cashing up and there were piles of copper and silver set out in rows on the counter.
"Caught one of 'em," the attendant said in triumph.
"I tell you I haven't done owt," Joby said again.
"Are you sure it was him?" the woman in the pay-box said, looking doubtfully at Joby.
Joby sensed she was sorry for him. He said, "He's got the wrong lad, but it's no use me telling him."
"Go on, clear off," the attendant said."And don't be so cheeky."
Joby turned away towards the entrance.
"I hope you get another pellet in your earhole when you get back inside," he said.
"Be off with you, you cheeky young devil, before I clatter your face."
The blind, daft, stupid old keff!

Look for:

- Words written in the way people speak rather that how they are correctly spelt. Underline or highlight these in one colour.
- Words that might only be used in one part of the country. Underline or highlight these in another colour. Talk about what they might mean.

People living in different parts of the country have their own special words. Sometimes they use ordinary words in a different way. A Scot, for example, might use 'no' instead of 'not': "You'll no be going out this time of night..."

This is not bad English. It is a special form of it, called dialect. Dialect is not the same as an accent. An accent is the way we pronounce words.

Work on a dialect dictionary. This could include words from where you live, or from a range of places including words from films and TV. Think about words your parents or grandparents use.

American English

Here is a dialogue between an American and a gang of troublemakers on the street.

> "OK, you wise guys, now listen good. I ain't gonna put up with no more brawling on the sidewalks. And no more fighting in the drug store either. If you wanna kill each other then do it someplace else, not on my territory."
>
> "Hey, man, that ain't fair! We're just havin a bit of fun."
>
> "Any more of your sorta fun and I'll shove the lot of you in the can and see that you stay there."

Use one colour to underline or highlight words written in the way the characters speak rather than how they are correctly spelt.

Use a different colour to show words or expressions that are American English.

Here are some American English words. Fill in the British English version. The first ones are done for you. Can you think of any more examples?

American English	British English
apartment	flat
mail	post
garbage	
diaper	
truck	
vacation	
potato chips	
french fries	
cab	

Imagine a British policeman is warning a street gang about their behaviour. Write out what he says to them.

Slang

This is part of Piers Davidson's gossip page from a pop magazine. It uses a great many slang expressions. Read through it and talk about what Piers is saying.

> Okay then bodies, a bit of most sorted news from the people in the know. A certain most extremely un-sad individual by the name of Wirral (yep, corrrrect it is HIM) has been bent down to pen push some wicked new books. Monsenior Wirral's new collection of romantic slosh (not!) will be available even as I scrawl these words.
>
> Utterly happenin' events are going down in London's east side, with MC Giles and his home boys. A most superb set of songs are coming hence from a rather suspicious sound studio down them ways – bodies have been telling me that we're looking at one un-un-un horrendous album later in the years. Me I'm still reeling from one missie going by the somewhat freaky initials of D A L (yes indeedy – her) and her freshest new collection 'What's the beef ?'. If that isn't one deal of an album I'm my own grandmother. Oops no more space. Byeeeeee!
>
> *Piers Davidson*

Make a list of slang expressions used in your school. Arrange them into alphabetical order and make a dictionary.

Write a piece of direct speech. Two people are talking about what they are going to do after school. Use some of the words from your list.

✂

Hello again. My first piece of news from a reliable source is that Wirral, known to us all from his popular acting roles, has completed a set of novels. These light fantasy books are available now.
Pop group 'MC Giles and the Home boys' are rumoured to be recording their second album. They are using an old studio in London's East End. The group should have the album finished shortly. The question is, will it be as good as D A L 's latest offering 'What's the beef?', a truly original and moving work. The End – Piers Davidson

5 Language patterns

This section looks at the more detailed structures of language, based on the working of the sentence. The concept of the sentence is fundamental, and it is dealt with on the first sheet. The parts of speech are studied in turn, and creative activities are suggested to provide practice in using them. Dry definitions or 'train-spotting' type exercises are pointless, and have been excluded unless there is no alternative. All the work is given a context in the real writing that students are doing. The importance of verbs is stressed with work on tense and person.

The debate over what grammatical knowledge should be taught continues to rage. Those who criticise 'poor grammar' often mean poor spelling and punctuation which, of course, is not grammar at all. The object of this section is to offer work on the irreducible core of material that is actually useful and within the grasp of students at key stage 3 working at the lower levels of attainment. The concepts of 'phrase' and 'clause' have been ignored as just too abstract and difficult for these students. Words such as 'qualify' and 'modify' in relation to parts of speech have been replaced by the less accurate, but much more easily understood, word 'describe'. 'Subject and object' is not mentioned even though distinctions such as who/whom depend on knowledge of this. It will be argued that such knowledge is valuable, and of course it is, but when we are working with average or below average students it is essential to a) prioritise b) avoid confusion c) provide work at which these students can succeed and d) offer a task relevant to the writing they are doing.

It is suggested that work on parts of speech is included when it is appropriate to the task in hand, and that the whole section should not be taught at once.

Using the worksheets

Is it a sentence?

Objective: To teach that a sentence contains a verb, begins with a capital letter and ends in a full stop.
Students: Class discussion followed by individual writing.
Notes: Listening is the most effective way to grasp what a sentence is. A sentence makes sense by itself – a non-sentence sounds unfinished.
Linked pages: Verbs 1 – What is a verb? p.96, Capital letters p.118, Punctuation 1 – Ends of sentences p.119.

Verbs 1
What is a verb?

Objective: To introduce the idea of verbs.
Students: Individual or class work.
Notes: The familiar definition of a 'doing' word uncomfortably excludes the most common verb, 'to be'. 'Doing and being' words might be a better definition.
Extension: Make a list of verbs appropriate to a particular scenario – 'Lost in Space', 'Down the Tunnel' and so on. Use the word list in a piece of writing. Make a list of verbs appropriate to the activities of a particular animal then use them in a descriptive poem.
Linked pages: Thesaurus p.30, Verbs 2 – Better choices p.97, Tenses 1 and 2 pp.106 and 107.

Verbs 2
Better choices

Objective: Finding correct and appropriate verbs.
Students: Group or classwork, followed by individual writing.
Notes: Recognition of errors needs aural reinforcement, and the passages must be read aloud to the students. Make it clear that the words chosen for the 'chase' writing can be changed – 'ran' to running or run and so on.
Linked pages: Verbs 1 – What is a verb? p.96, Thesaurus p.30.

Nouns 1
Abstract and concrete

Objective: To define nouns and distinguish between concrete and abstract.
Students: Individual work.

Notes: Work with the class as a whole to ensure that the abstract/concrete concept is fully understood.
Differentiation: The highlighting/cloze exercises can be done orally as a class or group.
Linked pages: Nouns 2 – Common and proper p.99, Thesaurus p.30.

Nouns 2

Common and proper

Objective: To distinguish between common and proper nouns.
Students: Individual or group work following a class discussion.
Notes: There are various anomalies connected with common and proper nouns, but people, places, titles, days and months cover most proper nouns.
Linked pages: Nouns 1 – Abstract and concrete p.98, Capital letters p.118.

Nouns 3

Abstract creatures

Objective: Further work on abstract nouns, using them for poetry writing.
Students: Individual work.
Notes: Talk through the 'sadness' creature before asking students to start writing. Ensure that they work through a brainstorming and drafting process before writing on the sheet.
Differentiation: Some students may need suggestions for the final creature: laughter, fear, laziness, greed are good options.
Linked pages: Thesaurus p.30, Brainstorming 2 p.5, Word pictures p.6, Poetry 1 – What am I? p.52.

Pronouns

Objective: To show how pronouns can take the place of nouns.
Students: Individual or group work following a class discussion.
Differentiation: This is quite a difficult exercise and the teacher might like to mark in the slash marks in advance.
Linked pages: Nouns 1 and 2 p.98 and 99, First person – Using 'I' p.108, Second person – Hey, you! p.109.

Adjectives

Objective: To work with adjectives.
Students: Class discussion followed by individual work.
Notes: The boxes of adjectives are a brainstorm device only. Stress that it is not necessary to use all of the adjectives in the boxes.
Linked pages: Thesaurus p.30.

Adverbs

Objective: To introduce and use adverbs.
Students: A class activity followed by individual writing.
Notes: The concept of adverbs is kept simple here and only when and how adverbs are considered. The adverb game is amusing and can be extended with the students own choice of adverbs.
Linked pages: Thesaurus p.30.

Prepositions

Objective: To work with prepositions.
Students: Class activity followed by individual/paired writing.
Notes: A preposition is easier to understand than define. A better definition than the one on the sheet is that they show relationships, but a simpler phrase has been preferred. The 'Jenny jumped' activity clearly shows what prepositions do in an amusing way.
Differentiation: Students can be asked to write three sentences only about the picture, each one using a different preposition.
Linked pages: Longer sentences 1 p.110.

Conjunctions

Objective: To work on conjunctions.
Students: Class discussion followed by individual or pair work.
Linked pages: Longer sentences 1 p.110.

Tenses 1

Past, present and future

Objective: To introduce the concept of past, present and future tenses.
Students: Class discussion followed by individual writing.

Notes: Students may need further examples of the use of tenses. Ask a student to carry out a simple task, such as opening the window. Before starting, the student should say:

I will open the window
While the task is under way, he/she will say
I am opening the window
When the task is concluded, he/she will say
I opened the window.

Further tenses, such as continuous present and future (I am opening and I will be opening) are not mentioned but should be accepted. The shall/will distinction is also not considered in these materials.
The second starter sentence is straightforward – running commentaries are always in the present tense. The future sentence is more difficult. The teacher might help start off the next sentence, using 'he will...' as the opening words.
Linked pages: Verbs 1 and 2 pp.96 and 97.

TENSES 2

YESTERDAY, TODAY AND TOMORROW

Objective: To use the past and future tenses in the form of a diary.
Students: Individual or pair work.
Notes: The second diary is telling the story of a day that went wrong. Ensure students realise this before they start.
Linked pages: Tenses 1 – Past, present and future p.106, Diary 1 and 2 pp.58 and 59.

FIRST PERSON

USING 'I'

Objective: To work on two approaches to first person writing – the 'true story' and the 'persona'.
Students: Class discussion followed by individual writing.
Notes: A persona is a mask that a writer assumes. Without necessarily using this word, students should be shown that writing using 'I' doesn't have to be about the actual writer. Use the extract from *Me Jane*.
Differentiation: Some students may find it difficult to get started on the poem and may welcome suggestions such as: I am/a snake/when I am hungry...
Linked pages: Poetry – I am p.55, Story telling – True stories p.12, Diary 1 and 2 pp.58 and 8, Personal writing p.59.

SECOND PERSON

HEY, YOU!

Objective: To use second person writing.
Students: Class discussion followed by individual work.
Notes: Second person writing does not have to include the word 'you'. Most instructions miss it out entirely – Shut the door! Sit down! Point out that the directions do not have to go on using the word you.
Extension: Curse poems are another entertaining use of the second person, but need to be kept under control:

I hate you!
You have a face like a baboon!
May your toes fall off,
Your hair drop out...etc.

Linked pages: Instructions 1 – Cassette recorder p.69, Instructions 2 – Feeding the pet p.70, Providing information 1 – Fire! p.71.

LONGER SENTENCES 1 AND 2

Objective: To show two ways of joining sentences – using conjunctions, prepositions, conjunctive adverbs and relative pronouns.
Students: Individual, group or oral classwork.
Notes: The grammatical reasoning behind these methods of joining sentences has not been mentioned as this will only confuse. Students need to develop an ear for possible ways to build sentences. The final block of sentences in Longer sentences 1 can be joined using various words. Talk through the different shades of meaning that arise when different words are substituted. Longer sentences 2 is a more challenging task, as the sentences need to be restructured. The who/whom problem arises here. If the teacher feels it is appropriate to explain the subject/object distinction, this is best done orally.
Linked pages: Is it a sentence? p.95, Conjunctions p.105, Prepositions p.104.

Is it a sentence?

A **sentence** is a group of words that make sense by themselves.

The man in street. = not a sentence

The man walked in the street. = a sentence

A sentence must begin with a capital letter and end in a full stop. It must include a verb (a doing or being word).

If these are sentences, tick the box. If they are not, add words to make them into sentences.

A beautiful sunny day in June. ☐

There were three horses in the field. ☐

A bright green sweater. ☐

Abby hated rats and mice. ☐

Dozens of different types of fish, fruit, and vegetables. ☐

Choose one of these verb boxes. Write five sentences, using one verb in each sentence. You can use the verbs in any order.

walked	was	am
ran	opened	go
stopped	looked	hope
shouted	waved	will
replied	closed	like

Verbs 1 – What is a verb?

No sentence is complete without a **verb**.

- A verb tells you what the thing or person in the sentence is doing:

  I **ran** down the path. I **stroked** the cat.

- Or what they are:

  You **are** a Martian. I **am** the cat.

- Some verbs can be in two parts:

  The cat **was sleeping**.

Find five verbs to fit in the gaps below. The first verb should begin with 'a', the second 'b', and so on. The first one is done for you.

a) We **approached** the house.

b) We **b** ______________________________ the house.

c) We **c** ______________________________ the house.

d) We **d** ______________________________ the house.

e) We **e** ______________________________ the house.

Read this passage.
In the first part the verbs are underlined.
In the second part you should underline the verbs.
In the third part the verbs are missed out. Fill the gaps with suitable ones.

The lion was sleeping when the men from the zoo approached it. When it heard the footsteps, it woke. The beast roared loudly. It wanted some breakfast!
The man with the tranquilliser gun crept forward. Just then the lion stood up and padded away into the trees.
"Run after it!" shouted the chief keeper.
The marksman slipped through the bushes and trotted after the lion. He was trying to aim the gun when the creature stopped, turned, and charged towards him. The man fired one shot then ran back towards the other men.

"Quick!" ________________ the keepers. The marksman ________________ down his gun and ________________ as fast as he could. The lion ________________ on him. He ________________ no chance. Just then the lion ________________ and ________________. The dart ________________. The man ________________ safe.

Verbs 2 - Better choices

In this passage, some of the verbs are wrong choices. Put a slash (/) through these verbs and write a better choice in the margin.

The big car swung round the corner and stooped. A big man went out of it. He crushed the pavement, stopped up the garden path, and banged on the door. A man weeping a vest and trousers opened it.

"Is you Brian Dixon?" asked the big man.
"Who wants to know?" ask the man in the vest suspiciously.
"I am from Littletrees Pools. I am delighted to tell you that you had won the jackpot prize."
The lucky winner blanked his eyes in amazement.
"How much?" he grasped.
"A million pounds."

In the next extract the verbs are not wrong, but they are not very interesting. Think of better ones and write them in the margin.

The great bird went up then moved down again. It had seen a rabbit moving in a field. The bird put out its talons and took the rabbit. It went off, moving its huge wings. Soon its young would be eating up the rabbit. Meanwhile, the bird went off again, looking with its sharp eyes, ready to go down to pick up another meal.

A man with a deadly secret is being chased by secret agents. Here are some verbs that might be used to describe what the man was doing. Add three more words to the list then write about the chase.

Ran ______________________________

puffed ______________________________

stumbled ______________________________

Nouns 1 – Abstract and concrete

Nouns are words that **name** things.

cat **car** **school** **Susie** **London**

They can name things that are not objects, such as feelings and ideas:

anger unhappiness tiredness love safety education

These are called **abstract** nouns.

Nouns that name objects you can touch, see, hear, taste or smell are called **concrete** nouns.

Underline the nouns in the first part of this passage. Use one colour for concrete nouns, and a different colour for abstract ones.

The sheriff sat at the bar, cleaning his gun in anger. He drank only water. He needed to keep a clear head.

Jed burst through the door. "They're comin', Bob! Cactus Pete and his mob. And they ain't looking for rest and relaxation and a night's sleep, either! Them dudes are after your blood!"

The story continues, but with the nouns missing. Write interesting ones in the gaps.

Sheriff Bob put his ______________ back together and loaded it with six ______________. "Leave this to me, ______________," he said. "I'm going to bring ______________ to this town. I'm going out into the ______________ to meet those ______________. If they don't turn around and get out of ______________, they'll meet their ______________ this very ______________,

What happens to Sheriff Bob? Finish off the story, then ask your partner to circle five nouns you have used.

Nouns 2 – Common and proper

Proper nouns are names for people, and places and things when you mean one in particular. They start with capital letters. Other nouns are called **common nouns**.

Months of the year and days of the week are proper nouns, but seasons are common nouns.

common nouns	**proper nouns**
girl	Kelly Smith
city	Liverpool
school	Greentown Community School
a prime minister	the Prime Minister
poem	The Charge of the Light Brigade
film	Star Wars
book	The Colour Purple
day	Wednesday
month	June

Some of the common nouns in this passage have a slash through them. In the margin, write proper nouns to take their place. Cross out 'a' and 'the' if you need to. Make sure to give them capital letters.

The girl attended a school in a city. A boy was her best friend. One day in a cold month they took a bus into the centre of the city to see a film. On the way they met a boy, who was in their class.

The film was good. Afterwards they went to a burger restaurant for cheeseburgers and fries. The girl picked up a copy of a newspaper that someone had left behind. There was a picture of a boy on the front page. 'Look!' gasped the girl. 'We saw him on the bus! It says he has run away from home!'

These nouns have been written entirely in capital letters. Rewrite them in lower case letters. Make sure that any proper nouns start with capital letters.

TEACHER	TUESDAY	CARPET
________	________	________
ROBERT	WOOLWORTHS	SUMMER
________	________	________

Nouns 3 – Abstract creatures

This poem is about **anger**. It imagines that anger is an animal in a zoo. Draw and write about a creature called **sadness**. Make up your own abstract noun creature for the last cage.

The first cage holds **anger**.
He is red skinned,
With long slashing claws
and hair like fire.
His eyes flash like razor blades.
He screams horribly and rattles the bars,
But no-one takes any notice of him.

This cage holds **sadness**.

This cage holds

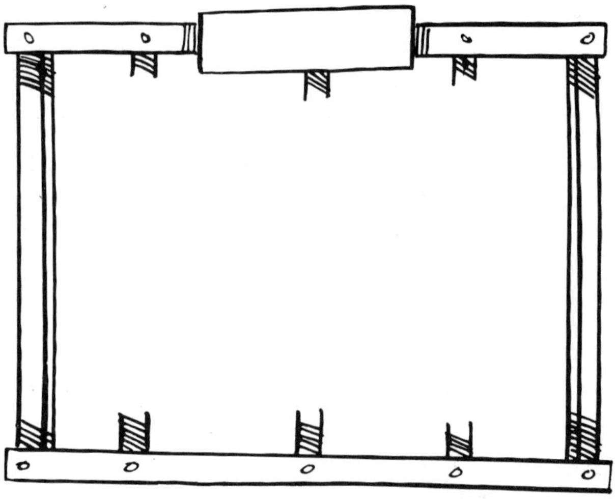

Pronouns

Pronouns take the place of nouns, They are used so that we don't have to keep repeating the noun every time we mention that person, place or thing.

John was fourteen. **He** enjoyed fishing.
Mum and Dad were angry. **They** glared at Henry.
Manchester is a great city. **It** now has a tramway system.
"Come here Scott! What are **you** doing!"
Here comes Mr Hammond with **his** dog.
This is 4C and this is **their** classroom.

Slash through the nouns that are repeated in these sentences. Write a pronoun in the margin.
There are some pronouns in the box below to help.

John was fourteen. John loved fishing. There was nothing John liked better than to sit by the river with John's sandwiches watching the wildlife. John never minded if John never caught anything.

The girls in the class were furious. The girls in the class didn't see why the girls in the class should have to stay in detention when it wasn't the girls in the class's fault. The broken window was nothing to do with the girls in the class.

The car refused to start. The car was old and worn out, and the car had obviously decided that the car had had enough. The car's battery was flat, and the car clearly wasn't going anywhere.

My name is Carl. Carl is twelve, and Carl goes to Longthorpe School. Carl's father is a business man and Carl's mother helps him part time. Carl has a new walkman that Carl is especially proud of. Carl's sister tries to borrow it, but Carl says "Clear off! That's Carl's!"

Pronoun box

He his hers mine my I her our
their they me we you yours it
she us them

Adjectives

In the first part of this passage the adjectives are underlined.

In the second part you should underline the adjectives.

In the third part the adjectives are missing. Write suitable ones in the gaps.

> **Adjectives** are words that tell you more about nouns.
>
> Here is a **green** box.
> Here is a **big** box.
> This box is **empty**.
> This **big green** box is **empty**.

The mysterious planet had a thick atmosphere that made it impossible to see the surface. The puzzled captain called in the ship's best scientist and asked a difficult question.

"What is that weird atmosphere made of? And why is it such a strange colour? I've never seen a blue planet before."

The scientist scratched his ________________ head. "I'm not sure.

But there is a(n) ________________ chance that this planet has

________________ chemicals. We may be on the verge of a(n)

________________ discovery."

Choose one of the boxes below and use the adjectives in a piece of writing. What are the adjectives describing? There is room for you to add more adjectives of your own before you start.

1	2
frightening	sweltering
dark	dry
terrifying	sleepy
dusty	baked
ancient	drooping
forgotten	thirsty
empty	

Adverbs

Adverbs are another sort of describing word. They tell us how and when.

The bus driver drove **fast.** Father **always** drove.
The teacher shouted **angrily**. The teacher **sometimes** shouted.
Steve **usually** overslept. Steve snored **noisily**.

Adverbs often end in 'ly', but not always. (Adjectives can end in 'ly' like ugly, or smelly.)

The adverb game

1 Cut out these adverbs.

silently

sadly

quickly

thoughtfully

angrily

fast

gracefully

clumsily

backwards

unusually

2 Put them in a box, (or a hat, if you have one!). Pick out an adverb and write it at the end of this sentence.

Walk across the room ____________________.

3 Take it in turns to carry out the instruction.

4 Now think of some adverbs of your own. Write them out and put them in the box.

You are going to write about a car chase. Which of these adverbs will be useful? Cross out any you cannot use, and add some new ones.

Adverbs box

noisily **dangerously** **always** **sometimes**
sleepily **carefully**

Prepositions

Prepositions show the position of one thing compared to another.

Jenny ran **over** the the road.
The train rumbled **through** the tunnel.
He shared his sandwich **with** an elephant.

Preposition box	
under	behind
before	for
up	by
down	over
in	round
out	on
off	through
with	

1 Jenny and the bus

Use the prepositions from the box in this sentence. Each time, talk about what the sentence means.

Jenny jumped ______________________ the bus.

2 Assault course

Look at this picture. Write about someone using this assault course. See how many prepositions you can use from the list in the box.

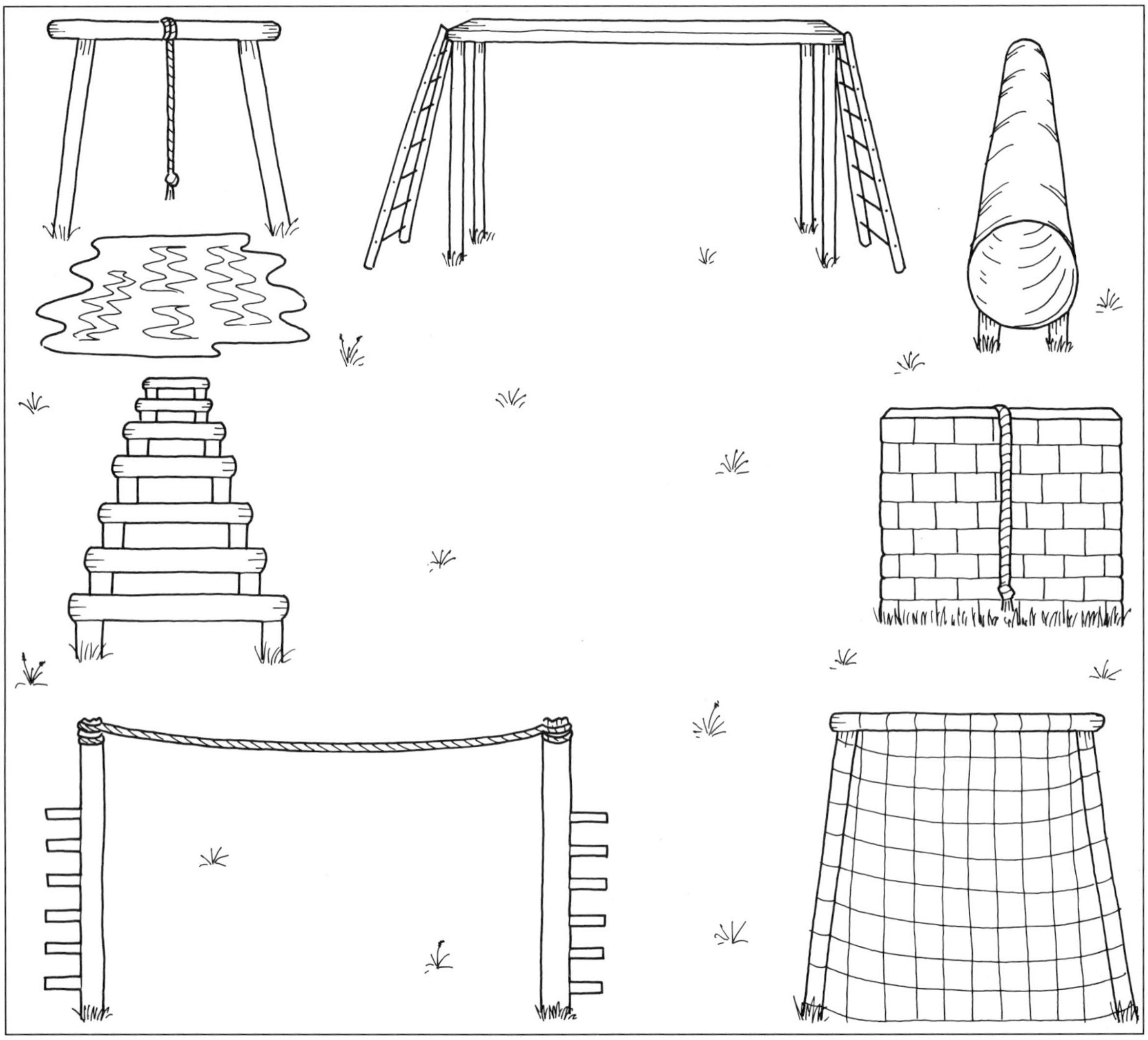

Conjunctions

Conjunctions are joining words.

John opened the box **and** took the money.
John opened the box **but** it was empty.
John took the money **when** he opened the box.
John needed money **so** he opened the box.

Here are some more conjunctions:

after **although** **as** **because** **but** **until** **before**
for **if** **so** **than** **unless** **when** **while**

In the first part of this passage the conjunctions are underlined.

In the second part the conjunctions are missing. Write suitable ones from the list in the box to fill in the gaps.

John needed cash very badly <u>so</u> he decided to borrow the coffee money. He was broke <u>because</u> he had spent all he had on a new pair of shoes <u>and</u> a silk shirt. He would get no more money <u>until</u> Thursday.

He knew it was wrong <u>but</u> he thought he would take a chance, <u>as</u> he was really desperate. He slipped into the office <u>after</u> everyone had gone ______ ______ opened the box. He was an honest person, ______ he really needed the money. He would put it back ______ he got paid.

______ he was putting the money into his pocket the door opened. It was the boss!

"Caught red handed!" he roared. "Money has gone missing a number of times, ______ now I have found the thief! Wait there ______ I call the police!"

Continue this story for a few more sentences. Pass your story over to a partner. Ask them to underline any conjunctions they find in what you have written.

Tenses 1 – Past, present and future

- Stories are usually written as if they happened in the past.

Karen **went** over to the fridge and **took** out an ice-cream.

- They can be written as if the events are happening now:

Karen **goes** over to the fridge and **takes** out an ice-cream.

- Or as if they haven't happened yet:

Karen **will go** over to the fridge and **will take** out an ice-cream.

We say that we are writing in the past, present or future **tense**.

Finish off these extracts with another sentence, keeping to the same tense.

John slipped and fell heavily on the wet pavement. Arnie was only a few metres behind.

"And Jackson is in second place as he rounds the last bend."

He will go mad when he sees that!

Tenses 2 - Yesterday, today and tomorrow

Here are two diary pages. On May 14th, the diary writer is thinking about a very special day tomorrow and is writing in the future tense. On the evening of May the 15th the same writer has had the exciting day, and is writing about what has happened. Finish off the diary entries.

Friday, May 14th

It'll be a great day tomorrow! There's going to be...

Saturday, May 15th

Today didn't turn out quite as I had expected!

First person – Using 'I'

Use **I**:

- when you are writing about things you did
- when you are pretending to be someone else.

(The poem below was not really written by a cat!)

1 Something you did

I missed the bus this morning and had to walk to school. I was really fed up as it was raining and I got soaked...

Finish off the writing about the wet morning, then write your own poem in the box. What sort of animal are you going to be?

2 Pretending to be someone or something

I am

A lazy cat.

On sunny days,

I stretch out in the shade

Wild as an African lion.

But when it is cold,

I am tame,

And hog all the fire

For myself!

I am

A

Second person – Hey, you!

When we speak directly to someone we can use the pronoun **you**. We can use it

- In a question:

What are **you** doing?

- When giving an order or instruction:

Get out of my garden, **you**!
You must start now.

- When giving information:

That's my foot **you**'re standing on!

Here are some directions. They are a mixture of instructions and information. Finish them off. There is a map to help.

To get to the station from here you should turn left at the Dog and Crook, then carry on until you get to the roundabout.

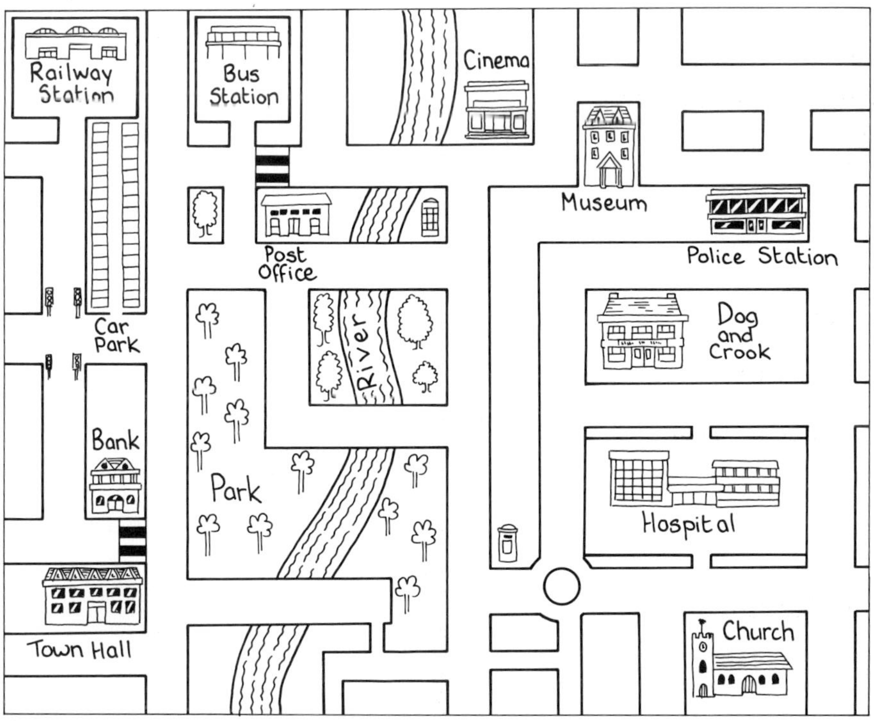

Longer sentences 1

Nothing but short sentences makes writing boring!

These sentences can be joined using the words in the word box. You may have to change the sentences. Write your new sentences in the spaces. The first two are done for you.

Word box
when
while
where
because
if
although
so
than
unless
after
before
as
since
until
but

1 a The tortoise is ill. He ate the the poisoned leaf.

b The tortoise is ill because he ate the poisoned leaf.

2 a Rose hadn't worked very hard. She passed the exam.

b Although Rose hadn't worked hard, she passed the exam.

3 a The boys met up. The trees hid them from the others.

b ______________________________

4 a The bus arrived. People in the queue were soaking wet.

b ______________________________

5 a The Head showed the parents round the school. 4c were having an angry debate.

b ______________________________

Choose one of the words from the box to fill the gaps in each of these sentences. Sometimes more than one word will fit. Compare your finished sentences with someone else's. Talk about how the meaning changes when you use different conjunctions.

Steve went to the garage ______________ the car had gone.

You can't get on the bus ______________ you have some money.

I'll give you ten pounds ______________ you pass your test.

He left the key under the mat ______________ that the plumber could get in.

Jake played much better ______________ the rest of the team.

Longer sentences 2

Lots of short sentences make writing boring!
These sentences can be joined together using **who**, **whom**, **whose** and **that**.

Join them up, using one of these words. The first two are done for you.

1 a John Smith is my grandfather. He is 60-years-old.

b John Smith, who is my grandfather, is 60-years-old.

2 a The car broke down in the street. It is running again.

b The car that broke down in the street is running again.

3 a I saw the black and white cat. It scratched me on Wednesday.

b ______________________________

4 a Karen Tyler was made form captain. I hate her.

b ______________________________

5 a The driver was very angry. Her car had been stolen.

b ______________________________

6 a The singers were a weird looking bunch. They made the record.

b ______________________________

7 a Here comes Bob. I hit him last week.

b ______________________________

8 a There are the visitors. They can't speak a word of English.

b ______________________________

Section 6

Proof reading

As in Section 5, Language patterns, this section concerns itself with the nuts and bolts of writing. The focus here, however, is on those items usually left to the proof reading stage – spelling, punctuation, agreement errors, headings.

Students should always be encouraged to write their ideas down in the first instance without stopping to check on difficult spellings or punctuation. Students with a problem in retention will have forgotten what they were going to say by the time they resume their work! There is a tendency among students to see proof reading as 'marking', i.e. the teacher's job. There will not always be a teacher around to do this, and the discipline of checking over work must be encouraged. It is not an easy task, and those students with problems of visual discrimination find it very difficult indeed. The activities suggested here should help. Throughout the book a simplified system of proof marks have been used, as detailed on the Proof reading marks worksheet.

Spelling is too big a topic to be tackled fully in a book such as this. It is, perhaps unfortunately, the aspect of writing skill that raises most hackles among critics of English teaching, and the one that seems to worry students the most. The reason for this is probably that, unlike areas such as style or structure, spelling is easily seen as 'right or wrong'. Students are anxious for similar reasons – spelling is something concrete to grasp amidst a mass of rather more abstract ideas.

The following points on spelling may be useful to teachers.

- Spelling is important at the proof reading stage but should not obsess students and teachers while the work is being drafted.
- The most effective tool for helping with spelling is the student's personal word bank, perhaps in the form of a spelling book.
- Spelling tests should be based on words that the students regularly misspell. Many spelling schemes use arbitrary lists of words designed to demonstrate a spelling rule, rather than test words that the students actually use and need.
- Be aware of subject specific vocabulary for science, technology and so on.
- Keep it positive – never teach spelling by asking students to pick the right word from a list of misspelt ones. Inevitably, they will learn the misspelt ones!
- Encourage the use of computer spelling checkers. These do not do the spelling for you, but actually reinforce spelling skills by offering a range of alternatives.
- Teaching homophones – fair, fare, wait, weight – together is generally a bad idea. Associating the words merely leads to extra confusion. Keep them apart – they should be attached to their meanings, not each other!
- A handful of homophones or near homophones are so common and so often confused that there is no alternative but to teach them together, plugging away until they are learnt. These are: there, their, they're; where, (were), wear; to, too, two. Also the have/of confusion in phrases such as 'I could of', and our/are.
- By and large, spelling rules are difficult to learn and loaded with exceptions. Better to learn the small list of regular errors than attempt to learn a raft of rules. Exceptions are the 'i before e' rule, with its useful and easily remembered rhyme, and the rule on double consonants. Double consonant errors represent a significant proportion of the total errors made.
- For many students, particularly those with a specific learning difficulty, spelling is such a major hurdle that they lose the confidence to tackle any writing at all. Spelling should be kept in proportion.

Using the worksheets

Proof reading marks

Objective: To provide a simple system of proof reading.

Students: Class discussion, followed by the checking exercise which can be individual, pair or group, or done orally as a class.

Notes: In general the materials in this book have avoided the trap of teaching by offering incorrect texts to be corrected. This approach reinforces the students own errors. This page is an exception, for fairly obvious reasons. Students will need plenty of practice in proof reading. Checking a partner's work rather than their own is a useful approach. (You may prefer to substitute your own system of proof marks following a discussion with the students.) The material in the box can be cut out and stuck inside the student's own workbook.

Spelling 1

Spotting mistakes

Objective: A demonstration of the principle of underlining words the writer is uncertain about rather than stopping to look them up.
Students: Individual or pairwork. Students can exchange their stories and check each others underlinings.
Notes: Underlining is not necessary when the work is being keyed in to a computer as the spelling checker will check every word. Students should learn that the computer cannot spot some of the common errors, such as there/their.
Differentiation: Some students will be confident in using a dictionary. Others may need some practice at this. The correct choice of dictionary is vital for students with special educational needs. There are a range of specialist 'spelling' dictionaries that make the process of looking up more straightforward.
Linked pages: Proof reading marks p.115, Spelling 2 – Word families p.117.

Spelling 2

Word families

Objective: To practise forming words with double consonants.
Students: This page is probably better looked at as a class.
Notes: The sheet could be set as a learning homework, following a discussion, and tested the next day. The important point to emphasise is listening – the long vowel in taped = single consonant, the short vowel in tapped = double consonant.

Capital letters

Objective: To practise using capital letters.
Students: Class discussion followed by individual, pair or group proof reading.
Notes: There are many anomalies in the use of capital letters; this page offers a reasonably simple formula. Uses such as The Headteacher/ the headteacher are very much a matter of taste. As *Fowler's Modern English Usage* puts it, 'Uniformity is lacking not only in practice but also in precept'.
Linked pages: Nouns 2 – Common and proper p.99, Is it a sentence? p.95.

Punctuation 1

Ends of sentences

Objective: To give practice in using full stops, exclamation marks, question marks.
Students: Individual or class work.
Notes: A straightforward exercise. The most common error is that students do not always put end punctuation inside speech marks.
Linked pages: Punctuation 4 – "and" p.122.

Punctuation 2

Commas

Objective: To demonstrate the use (and over use) of the comma.
Students: The first passage should be read silently. The second reading is best done by the teacher. The proof reading exercise can be done individually or in groups.
Notes: The use of commas is very much down to listening to the flow of language. Some students find this difficult. It is worth reading the second passage aloud to students before asking them to tackle the proof reading.
Linked pages: Punctuation 1 and 3 pp.119 and 121.

Punctuation 3

Semi-colons, colons and dashes

Objective: Work on these punctuation marks.
Students: Talking as a class or in groups, followed by a group or individual exercise.
Notes: These are difficult marks for students to use and this page is just a brief introduction. The final text should be given out after the main page has been collected in.
Linked pages: Punctuation 1 and 2 pp.119 and 120.

Punctuation 4

"And"

Objective: To punctuate direct speech.
Students: Class discussion followed by individual writing.
Notes: One way to show that speech marks enclose only the words actually spoken is to ask students to highlight the spoken words, using different colours for each character.
Differentiation: The final exercise could be based on a short improvised conversation in pairs which is then written up.
Linked pages: Direct speech p.48.

Punctuation 5

Apostrophes

Objective: To show that the apostrophe takes the place of missing letters.
Students: Individual, pair or group work.
Notes: 'Apostrophes for missing letters' is a reasonably straightforward matter, and words such as aren't and he's should be learnt as words. Students may be amused to know that one word – fo'c's'le – should, to be correctly written, have three apostrophes! The problem word is its/it's and this has a page to itself.
Linked pages: Punctuation 6 and 7 pp.124 and 125.

Punctuation 6

More apostrophes

Objective: Work on the possessive apostrophe.
Students: Individual, pair or group work.
Notes: The rules for apostrophes showing possession are a minefield, and many now feel that the best thing would be to abandon them altogether. In general, the problem is less with missing apostrophes than with apostrophes over-enthusiastically applied, as so often seen on the greengrocer's barrow. The problem with teaching apostrophes is that it reminds students of them and then they use them where they are not needed. This page attempts to offer a clear and straightforward set of rules. The topic will need much reinforcement.
Linked pages: Punctuation 5 and 7 pp.123 and 125, Plurals p.126.

Punctuation 7

Its and It's

Objective: To discriminate between its and it's.
Students: Group discussion followed by an exercise that can be individual or group.
Notes: Its adds more confusion to the apostrophe problem by not having one even though it shows possession. The simple rule to offer is 'use *its* unless it is short for *it is*'.
Linked pages: Punctuation 5 p.123.

Plurals

Objective: To work on irregular plurals.
Students: Individual or group work. The information box can be pasted into work books.
Notes: Irregular plurals are best taught as they occur. Some rules are sufficiently constant to make them worth learning. Others, such as words ending in 'o', are hopelessly irregular.
Linked pages: Punctuation 6 – p.124.

Do we agree?

Objective: To work on verb agreement.
Students: Individual or group work.
Notes: Confusion mainly arises when the subject is a group – the class are waiting sounds correct, although the class is waiting is considered correct. The former may well end up as standard usage before long. When the action described suggests that the members of the group are acting as individuals the plural use is probably to be preferred – the class are fighting one another. In the passage, the government is to blame is correct, as the government is in this sense a single entity.
Linked pages: Verbs 1 and 2 pp.96 and 97.

Headings

Objective: To work on headings and sub-headings.
Students: Individual or group work.
Notes: Effective organisation of writing with headings, paragraph numbers, and so on is an important skill. Further reinforcement can come from looking at text books from various subjects to see how they are organised.
Linked pages: Desk top publishing p.132.

Proof reading marks

When we check over a piece of work, we use special marks when we find mistakes. Here are some of the most useful ones.

With the writing

Put a slash (/) through any words to be cut out.
Underline any words that should be changed.
Use a ʌ to show where something is missing.
Put a circle around punctuation that should be changed or is missing.
Use a [to show where a new paragraph should start.

In the margin

Write in what you want changed. You can use these signs and abbreviations:
cap = change to capital letter
l.c. = change to lower case (small letters)
n.p. = new paragraph

Someone has started to proof read this piece of writing, but hasn't finished it. Correct it using the information in the box.

The Professor was very angr ʌ indeed. no-one took — angry
his theory seriously. "If nothing is is done, the — (")
world is doomed," he raged to his assant. The — assistant
comet will strik ʌ th ʌ planet earth in the year 2045 — strike the (.)
we must planning now to save the wrold. We will
need rockets. and atomic weapons to destroy the
comet before we ourselves are destryed! His
assistant, Horace, tried to soothe his boss. Don
worry boss, they'll believe you when publish your
results. They'll have to beleve you, or we're all
doomed!" The professor to his telescope. "There's
no doubt at at all!" he said grimly. "It's hedding
straight for us!"

Spelling 1 – Spotting mistakes

Here is the beginning of Jane's story. She was not sure how to spell some of the words, so she has underlined so that she can check them after she has finished. It is better to do this than to look up a word as you go along, in case you forget what you were going to say.

Is Jane's spelling right or wrong? Check the underlined words, using a dictionary. If they are wrong, put the correct spelling in the margin. When you have done that, continue the story and underline any words you are not sure about. Check them when you have finished.

It was a wild and stormy night. Sue was trying to get to sleep, but the <u>wailing</u> of the wind in the <u>chimeny</u> kept her awake.

There was a <u>suden</u> <u>rattle</u> of stones at the window. She got up and put on her dressing gown. She looked out of the window and saw her best <u>freind</u> Julie looking up at her.

"You've got to get dressed and come <u>quickly</u>," said Julie in a loud <u>wisper</u>. "Chris is in big <u>trouble</u>, and only you and I can do something about it!"

Spelling 2 - Word families

We can add letters to the beginning and end of words to make them into word families.

▪ When we add endings like 'ing' to a word, we sometimes need to add an extra letter.

key word	**fit**
adding at the beginning	**refit misfit unfit**
adding at the end	**fitting**
or at the beginning and end	**refitted**

let **letting**
tap **tapping** **tapped**
scrap **scrapping** **scrappy** **scrapped**
rot **rotting** **rotted**

but not when the key word ends in 'e':

tape **taping** **taped**
scrape **scraping** **scraped**

▪ You can add endings to key words ending in 'y' such as:

buy **buying**
play **playing** **played**

but not always when the ending is 'ed'. Learn these:

cry **cried** pay **paid** say **said** lay **laid**

Make word families starting with these key words.

start

dry

pay

make

stare

Capital letters

What has a **capital letter**?

- The beginning of a sentence.
- Names of people, places, titles (such as books, films, TV programmes), days of the week and months.
- 'I' when it stands by itself.
- The start of a new piece of speech.
- Initials.
- Sometimes the first letter in each line of a poem has a capital letter.

Capital letters	**Lower case letters**
Fred Jones	a chap from our street
Mickey Mouse	a mouse
Bournemouth	a seaside town
June	summer
RSPCA	
Wednesday	

Proof read this passage for capital letters. Underline the lower case letter and write **cap** in the margin.

the laboratory door slammed back as dr martin burst into the room. he was obviously very excited.

"this discovery will amaze the world! no-one, not even professor smith in canada, has come up with anything as good as i have found."

he was obviously very excited. his assistant tried to calm him down. "tell me all about it, dr martin" he said.

"certainly, john," beamed dr martin. "i took gold and platinum, and exposed them to those new rays we have been working on. look! the mercury and platinum have changed into other elements! They have turned into iron and copper!"

"but dr martin," objected john, "iron and copper aren't worth as much as gold and platinum."

"oh dear," said dr martin. "i never thought of that."

Punctuation 1 – Ends of sentences

. ? !

These three signs mark the **end** of a sentence. Use a full stop unless the sentence is:

- a question (use **?**)
- an exclamation or especially forceful sentence (use **!**).

(An exclamation is something that people say when they are angry, surprised, or upset. It doesn't have to be part of a sentence.)

Be careful not to use too many exclamation marks. Keep them only for very forceful sentences and never use more than one.

Read this passage. Talk about the full stops, question marks and exclamation marks, and why they are used. Notice that these marks are written **inside** the speech marks.

> "Good grief!" laughed Tricia. "Whatever do you look like?"
>
> Robert certainly looked a mess. His face was spattered with jam. More jam was splattered on to his shirt.
>
> "Don't laugh!" he shouted angrily. "How would you like it?"
>
> Tricia wouldn't like it. She was very puzzled. However had he got into that state?

Fill in the punctuation at the end of the sentences in this passage.

> Henry was obviously upset ☐ "Shut up ☐ " he yelled, waving his arms in the air ☐ "What are you laughing about ☐ Just clear off ☐ "
>
> The others soon realised that Henry was close to tears and stopped laughing. "We're sorry we laughed," said Judy ☐ "What's the matter ☐ "

Choose one of the two passages above and continue it. Take special care with the full stops, commas and exclamation marks.

Punctuation 2 – Commas

What job do **commas** do?

- They break up long sentences to make them easier to follow.
- They separate things on a list.
- If you are reading aloud they show you where to pause.

Warning! Don't over-use commas. Think – would a full stop be better?

Read this passage silently, then aloud. The writer forgot to use any commas!

> It was a beautiful summer's day. The sun was shining the birds were singing and the trees looked at their best. The boys decided to spend a few days camping. They got together their tent sleeping bags groundsheet a small gas stove a kettle and a supply of food and set off on their bikes wondering what adventures they would have.

Now proof read the passage. Put in the missing commas and draw a circle round them.

The next passage has too many commas. Find ways to join the short sentences into longer ones. Use proof reading marks to make your changes.

> Crocodiles are reptiles, they have a tough, armoured skin, they vary in size from five feet long to 20 feet long, they have their eyes, ears, and nose at the top of their heads, they can lie submerged in the water and keep watch, they lay up to 90 eggs in a nest, sometimes the nest is made of dead plants, sometimes the nest is buried in the sand,

It was a beautiful summer's day. The sun was shining, the birds were singing, and the trees looked at their best. The boys decided to spend a few days camping. They got together their tent, sleeping bags, groundsheet, a small gas stove, a kettle and a supply of food and set off on their bikes, wondering what adventures they would have.

Punctuation 3 – Semi-colons, colons and dashes

; is a **semi-colon**. It is half way between a comma and a full stop and is used for longer pauses inside a sentence.

: is a **colon**. Is is used to introduce a list or a quotation (writing out words taken from somewhere else).

- is a **dash**. We use dashes to mark out words that are not really part of the sentence we are writing.

Read this passage. Look for the semi-colons, colons and dashes and talk about the job they are doing.

Great Britain is made up of three countries: England, Scotland and Wales. Many people think that Northern Ireland is part of Great Britain; this is not so. Northern Ireland is a separate province. Great Britain – also called the United Kingdom or UK – is a member of the European Community. The European Community – formerly known as the common market – has been described in these words: "The most important development in European history in the 20th century". This is probably true; not everyone agrees, however!

✂

This is a copy of the passage you have just seen, but with the semi-colons (;) colons (:) and dashes (–) missed out. Put them back by writing them in the circles.

Great Britain is made up of three countries ○ England, Scotland and Wales. Many people think that Northern Ireland is part of Great Britain ○ this is not so. Northern Ireland is a separate province. Great Britain ○ also called the United Kingdom or UK ○ is a member of the European Community. The European Community ○ formerly known as the common market ○ has been described in these words ○ "The most important development in European history in the 20th century". This is probably true ○ not everyone agrees, however!

Punctuation 4 – "and"

Speech marks are used to show the words that people actually say, in a story or other piece of writing.

Mike was sitting in the garden with his feet up reading a book.
"Hello," called Jean. She came in through the gate.
"Well, if it isn't Jean!" said Mike, very surprised. "What are you doing round here? I thought you lived on the other side of town!"
Just then Sue, Mike's sister, looked through the window.
"Hi, Jean! come on in!"
"I thought you had come to see me!" said Mike, laughing.
Jean laughed and said "Not a chance!"

Points to note:

- Speech marks show only the words that are actually spoken.
- Punctuation goes inside the speech marks.
- When a new speaker starts speaking, a new paragraph is started, unless...
- The words spoken do not start a sentence. (Jean laughed and said "Not a chance!")

Write a short conversation. You could carry on with the story above or invent a new one.

Punctuation 5 – Apostrophes

One use of the **apostrophe** is to show where letters are missing.
We miss out letters when we join two words together.

are not = aren't
is not = isn't
she is = she's

Shorten these word pairs, making sure the apostrophe goes in where the letters are missing.

he is = ______________________

is not = ______________________

they have = ______________________

have not = ______________________

shall not = ______________________

can not (cannot) = ______________________

I will = ______________________

you will = ______________________

had not = ______________________

could not = ______________________

It is = ______________________

they are = ______________________

I am = ______________________

will not = ______________________

Write some sentences of your own
using the words pairs you have worked on. The first is done for you.

"**I'm** not wasting my time on people who **can't** be bothered to say thank you," grumbled Mr Potts.

Apostrophes can be used to show when people miss out letters in speech. What letters has Ted missed out here?

"I'm not goin' anywhere," said Ted. "I'm quite 'appy where I am."

Write another sentence that might be spoken by Ted.

____

____

____

____

____

Punctuation 6 – More apostrophes

- One use of an **apostrophe** is to show when something belongs to someone or something. We add an apostrophe and an s.

  This drink belongs to Mick. This is **Mick's** drink
  That is the battery from our car. That is our **car's** battery
  I was not impressed with the speech of the Prime Minister. I was not impressed with the **Prime Minister's** speech.

- When the person or thing doing the belonging is plural, we just add an apostrophe and no extra s.

  Here are the changing rooms of the girls. Here are the **girls'** changing rooms.
  He stole the hubcaps of the cars. He stole the **cars'** hubcaps.

- Remember that just because there is an s at the end of a word, it doesn't mean we add an apostrophe. An apostrophe shows **belonging** – **Fred's** hat, the **dog's** dinner.

- Don't use an apostrophe when the s is there because the word is a plural – the **carrots** were delicious, the **desks** were untidy.

Explain the difference between: trees tree's trees'.

In the words below the apostrophe shows **belonging**. Make up sentences using the words. Watch out for singular (dog's = 1 dog) and plural (dogs' = more than 1 dog).

John's ____

____

computer's ____

____

elephants' ____

____

policeman's ____

____

school's ____

____

teachers' ____

____

Punctuation 7 – Its and it's

A teacher's complaint

I really hate my pupils,
They always give me fits,
By writing **it's** when they mean **its**
And spelling **its** as **it's**!

Its and it's can be very confusing, but the rule is very simple!

It's is only used to make **it is**, or **it has**, short. The apostrophe shows that letters are missing.

It's a lovely day = It is a lovely day

What a pity it's worn out = ______________________

It's got a green face = ______________________

Its means that something **belongs** to it

This is the car, and that is **its** engine.

Read this short passage. Look for it's and its and talk about why they are used.

> "It's very sad that the old car has come to its final resting place," said old Jake. "It's been a real friend to me, and it's never let me down. I shall miss its friendly face and its cheerful roar."
> "It's only got a roar because of the hole in its exhaust," laughed Ted. "Call that a car! It's falling to bits!"

Put its or it's in the spaces.

"When you meet the dragon, watch out for __________ tail. __________ very likely to swipe you with it if __________ in a bad mood. And don't forget __________ got a nasty habit of opening __________ mouth and frying you with __________ breath. __________ a good idea to creep up on him when __________ raining. A dragon hates getting __________ scales wet."

Plurals

We usually make a word into a **plural** by adding an **s** on the end:

dog↔dogs **computer↔computers**

But words ending in **s**, **x**, **ch**, or **sh** need **es** to make them plural:

boss↔bosses **kiss↔kisses** **box↔boxes** **church↔churches** **dish↔dishes**

For most words ending in **f** or **fe** change the **f** to a **v** and add **es**:

half↔halves **life↔lives** **knife↔knives** **leaf↔leaves**

(But some, such as roof and chief, just need an **s** – roofs, chiefs.)

Words ending in **y** just need an **s**:

day↔days **play↔plays** **toy↔toys**

Unless there isn't a vowel in front of the **y**, when we change the **y** to an **i** and add **es**:

flies **hobbies** **jellies**

Words ending in **o** sometimes need just an **s**:

piano↔pianos **loo↔loos** **kangaroo↔kangaroos**

But some need **es**:

cargo↔cargoes **potato↔potatoes** **volcano↔volcanoes** **go↔goes** **torpeo↔torpedoes**

Some words don't change at all:

fish **deer** **sheep**

While some have special plurals:

child↔children **mouse↔mice** **tooth↔teeth** **man↔men** **foot↔feet**

Write in the plurals for these words. The answers to some of them are in the box above.

try ____________________ leaf ____________________

hobby ____________________ tax ____________________

goose ____________________ sausage ____________________

calf ____________________ woman ____________________

tray ____________________ blackberry ____________________

potato ____________________ knife ____________________

Do we agree?

Verbs change when they talk about plural things.

The boy **is** asleep. The boys **are** asleep.
The teacher **was** annoyed. The teachers **were** annoyed.
The girl **plays** well. The girls **play** well.

Sometimes it is not clear whether we are talking about a singular or plural thing.
One of our space-ships **is** missing. (We are only talking about one spaceship.)
This class **is** brilliant. (We are talking about one class, even though there is more than one pupil in it.)
Pupils in that class **are** hopeless. (We are talking about lots of pupils.)

Choose the correct words to fill in the gaps. Put a slash (/) through the wrong word. The first two are done for you.

The cat ~~love~~/loves chicken.

One of the teachers was/~~were~~ ill.

Members of parliament is/are well paid.

This group is/are the best.

"And the British team wins/win the relay!"

The boys in this group is/are not so good.

The fleet have/has been sunk.

The council is/are working on the problem.

There was/were complaints about the food.

There was/were a letter on the mat.

Find words to fill in the gaps in this newspaper report.

Young criminal in sentence uproar

Mark Trimble, (18) ____________ sentenced to three months youth custody yesterday, but there ____________ protests from his victims. One of them ____________ Mrs Joan Smithers, whose savings ____________ stolen.

"Short sentences like this ____________ a big mistake," said Mrs Smithers. "I think much more should be done to help the victims of crime, who ____________ often forgotten by society. My savings ____________ gone, and the government ____________ to blame."

A police spokesperson said there ____________ fresh hopes that the missing money would be found.

Headings

Here is part of a brochure for Highscore School.

Highscore School Information

Science

Staff All the staff are brilliant scientists and hard working teachers. Dr X Plosion is Head of Department.

Laboratories The school has four, fully-equipped laboratories.

Safety Safety is our first priority and all pupils are instructed on this aspect of laboratory work.

Results 80% of pupils pass exams with grade C or better.

PE

Staff

Facilities

Safety

School sporting success

This brochure makes use of headings. There is a **main heading** (Highscore School Information) and **sub-headings** (Science and PE). These sections have their own sub-headings – staff, facilities and so on.

Make up the PE entries.
Headings and sub-headings are shown in print by using larger type size, or **bold** type. In your writing you can underline your headings.
Sometimes it helps to give your sub-headings numbers.

The paragraphs of a book review might have headings. Here are some possible ones:

- **The story** ▪ **The characters** ▪ **What I liked**
- **What I didn't like** ▪ **Suitability** (what sort of person would like this sort of book) ▪ **My conclusion.**

Talk about any sub-headings that might be included. Choose a book you have read and write a review using headings.

Section 7 Section

Word processing

Word processing is an important skill, but many students (and adults!) are put off by its apparent complexity. These pages offer practice in the basic skills of loading and saving, printing, simple text handling and use of the spelling checker when it is available. There are many word processing programs in use in school, and no one book can explain the detail of each one. These pages are appropriate for all systems, from the most basic to the highly sophisticated. An important principle is that a student does not need to know how it all works before being able to carry out some useful word processing. Skills are added as they are required.

Important note on the pages: The work here requires the teacher to key in and save the raw texts for the students to work on in advance. The following points on word processing may be useful to teachers.

- Few schools will be able to offer one machine per student. The teacher will need to be aware of 'fair turns' and organise sessions so that some students will be working on planning and drafting while others will be producing final copies on the word processor.
- Encourage students to tackle short pieces of work, such as poems, to begin with.
- Pair and group work is obviously better in terms of keyboard time, and these pages are designed with this in mind. The co-operative element and discussion work which results can lead to the enhancement of skills and ideas.

Using the worksheets

Word processing 1

Keying in text

Objective: Simple word processing – loading, saving, keyboarding, printing, inserting and deleting text. Use of the spelling checker.
Students: Pair or group work.
Notes: Key in, save and back up the raw text 'Grave' for the students to work on.
Linked pages: Thesaurus p.30, Word processing 2 – Making corrections p.131, Desk top publishing p.132.

Word processing 2

Making corrections

Objective: More sophisticated text handling.
Students: Pair or group work.
Notes: Key in, save and back up the raw text 'Meeting' for the students to work on.
Linked pages: Proof reading marks p.115, Word processing 1 – Keying in text p.130, Desk top publishing p.132.

Desk top publishing

Objective: To introduce some of the vocabulary and skills of DTP.
Students: Pair or group work.
Notes: This is a fairly sophisticated task. Many DTP packages used in school, however, can be quite simple. Start by encouraging students to play with the system, learning as they go.
Linked pages: Word processing 1 and 2 pp.130 and 131.

Word processing 1 – Keying in text

This passage has missing words. In pairs or groups, talk about the best choice of words for the passage.

There was a ________________ glow of ________________ from the graveyard. As Peter and Stacey got ________________, they saw ________________ shadows cast on the ________________ of the church – shadows of two ________________. The shadows bent and ________________, and bent again.

They could hear the ________________ of shovels ________________ into the loose ________________, and a ________________ noise when they hit a stone.

The ________________ children ________________ nearer. Soon they heard the ________________ sound of a shovel ________________ wood. The ________________ stopped. There was a short ________________, then the noise of ________________ wood.

Now sit round the computer. Make sure that your word processing program is loaded and that everything is powered up and ready.

Load the file 'Grave' into the word processor. Move the cursor to the first space. One person should read out the chosen words and another should type the word in. Do not get impatient if the typist is slow. No one else should touch the keyboard. When you have typed in a word, delete the blank line.

Now work through the passage, filling in all the spaces with your chosen words.

When you have done this you should:

- Run your work through a spelling checker, if you have one.
- Decide on layout, type size and font if you are using a desk top publishing system.
- Save your work using a different file name.
- Make sure your printer is on line, then print out your work.

Original version of the passage:

There was a faint glow of light from the graveyard. As Peter and Stacey got closer, they saw huge shadows cast on the wall of the church – shadows of two men. The shadows bent and jerked, and bent again.

They could hear the sound of shovels digging into the loose soil, and a clanking noise when they hit a stone.

The horrified children crept nearer. Soon they heard the hollow sound of a shovel hitting wood. The digging stopped. There was a short silence, then the noise of splintering wood.

Word processing 2 – Making corrections

The author has started to proof read this passage. The mistakes have been marked, but not yet corrected.

Working together to finish off the proof reading, write the corrections in the margin.

Now load the file 'Meeting'. Use your copy to correct the work on screen. When you have finished you should:

- Run the work through a spelling checker to see if you have missed anything.
- Decide on layout, type size and font if you are using a desk top publishing system.
- Save your work using a different file name.
- Check your printer is on line, then print out your work.

The meeting

Karen was siting on a bench in the park, eating her sandwiches and watching the world go by. She hardly noticed the person who came and sat on the same seat. She was miles away, thinking of her forthcoming holiday in spain next week.

The other person on the bench coghed, and Karen glanced round. small, white face was wrapped in a red colored face scarf – and it was a fase she knew!

The newcomer looked at Karen and she, to, showed recognition in her face, although she didn't seem pleased to be recognised. Carly exclaimed Karen. "I haven't seen you since we left school!"

"Hello Karen." Carly seemed embarased to be recognised, and Karen could see why. Her clothes are ragged, she wore a filthy pair of trainers on feet, she looked as if the bench they were sitting on was her only bed.

karen didn't know what to say. "How are you" seemed a stupid question as Carly obviously wasn't well at all. She couldn't ask "What are you doing now" either.

"I must go" said Carly, but Karen stoped her. "Stay for a minute. Have a sanwich, I've got lots."

"I got plenty of food of my own," said Carly, but she looked at the sandwiches as if she hadn't eaten for weeks.

Desk top publishing

Munchester Leisure Centre needed a new leaflet. The manager wrote out what he wanted to say, then asked someone with a DTP (desk top publishing) system to design it. The result is in the box.

What the manager wrote:

```
Visit Munchester Leisure Centre!
At Munchester Leisure Centre you will find activities for
all the family such as swimming (two heated pools), fitness
training, aerobics, indoor tennis and badminton and many
more. Charges are reasonable, and young children are free!
Visit us now.
Munchester Leisure Centre. Park Rd, MUNCHESTER MU22 7LT
telephone 01276 363636
```

What the DTP designer came up with.

> ## Visit Munchester Leisure Centre!
>
> At **Munchester Leisure Centre** you will find activities for *all* the family such as
>
> - swimming (two heated pools)
> - fitness training
> - aerobics
> - indoor tennis and badminton
>
> and many more. Charges are reasonable, and young children are *free*!
>
> **Visit us now!**
>
> **Munchester Leisure Centre. Park Rd, MUNCHESTER MU22 7LT**
>
> **☎ 01276 363636**

The **DTP designer** used

- different fonts like this
- italics *like this*
- bold type **like this**
- different point sizes like these:

ten point twelve point eighteen point

- special symbols or dingbats like these:

● (bullet point)

☎ (telephone)

special frames.

Find out how to carry out these tasks on your school DTP system. Design a leaflet like the one for the leisure centre. Remember that using too many changes of font makes the final leaflet look unattractive and messy.

Assessment 1 - Flowchart

Name ______________________ **Date** ______________

Work done ______________________________

Did you work:

with a group? by yourself?

With a group:

How well did you work together?

What problems were there?

How could you work together better in the future?

By yourself:

How much help did you need?

Would you have prefered to work with a partner? Why?

How do you feel about the work you have done?

pleased? not satisfied?

Pleased:

Why are you pleased with your work?

Not satisfied:

How could you have improved the work you have done?

What have you learnt by doing this work? (Carry on writing over the page.)

What writing skills do you need/want to work on next?

Assessment 2 - Poems

Name ______________________ **Date** ______________

Work done ______________________________

Is there a special pattern, such as rhyme, or a special number of lines or syllables?

Yes ☐ No ☐

If you have answered 'yes', what is the pattern?

What words do you especially like in the poem?

Did the poem sound good when you read it aloud?

Yes ☐ Not specially ☐

Does the poem use interesting word pictures and comparisons? If so, copy out the best one.

What **one thing** would most improve the poem?

Partner's report on the poem.

Assessment 3 - Stories

Name ______________________ **Date** __________

Name of author ______________________

Title of story ______________________

Read your story through then answer these questions.
What type of story is it?

Horror ☐ Science fiction ☐ Adventure ☐ Crime ☐ Real life ☐

Other ______________________

Does the story have a good **plot** with a beginning, a middle and an end?

Good ☐ Average ☐ Not good ☐

Does it have a good **climax**?

Good ☐ Average ☐ Not good ☐

Who is the most interesting character in the story?

____

Why?

____

____

____

____

____

What **one thing** would most improve the story?

____

____

____

____

____

Partner's report on the story.

____

____

____

____

____

Assessment 4 - Factual writing

Name ______________________ **Date** ____________

Name of author ______________________

Subject of the piece of writing ______________________

How well do you think the information is organised?

Very well ☐ Quite well ☐ Not very well ☐

Is the writing broken up into paragraphs?

Yes ☐ No ☐

Are headings used in the writing?

Yes ☐ No ☐

List two important facts from the writing

1 ______________________

____

____

2 ______________________

____

____

Does the writing express opinions?

Yes ☐ No ☐

If so, what are they?

____

____

____

____

What **one thing** would improve the piece of writing?

____

____

____

____

Partner's report on the writing.

____

____

____

____